Illuminate
Publishing

WJEC
GCSE Food and
Home Nutrition
Economics

Bethan Jones • Victoria Ellis

Published in 2013 by Illuminate Publishing Ltd, P.O. Box 1160,
Cheltenham, Gloucestershire GL50 9RW

Orders: Please visit www.illuminatepublishing.com
or email sales@illuminatepublishing.com

British Library Cataloguing in Publication Data

A catalogue record for this book is available from the British Library

ISBN 978-1-908682-13-0

Printed by Ashford Colour Press Ltd., Gosport, Hampshire.

09.13

The publisher's policy is to use papers that are natural, renewable and
recyclable products made from wood grown in sustainable forests. The
logging and manufacturing processes are expected to conform to the
environmental regulations of the country of origin.

Every effort has been made to contact copyright holders of material
produced in this book. If notified, the publisher will be pleased to rectify
any errors or omissions at the earliest opportunity.

This material has been endorsed by WJEC and offers high quality
support for the delivery of WJEC qualifications. While this material has
been through a WJEC quality assurance process, all responsibility for
the content remains with the publisher.

Editor: Geoff Tuttle
Design and layout: Nigel Harriss

Image Credits:

Cover image: © Shutterstock / Steve Mann

Editorial images © Shutterstock

Acknowledgements:

The authors and publisher would like to thank:

Jessica Davies and Rachel Rogers for their detailed reviews and expert
insights and observations.

Students at Cwmtawe Community School, Swansea for their excellent
photographs.

Dedication:

To the many teachers who have shown such dedication and enthusi-
asm for this course and routinely share good practice and resources
with their peers.

Contents

Introduction

This book has been written for the WJEC GCSE Home Economics: Food and Nutrition course. It has been tailored to match the qualification specification and to help guide you through the requirements of the course.

The Food and Nutrition course is divided into two parts:
Unit 1: Principles of Food and Nutrition
Unit 2: Controlled Assessment

Unit 1: Principles of Food and Nutrition contains all the underpinning knowledge you will need to understand the subject. This will also prepare you for the written examination and apply theory to practice in the Controlled Assessments.

Unit 2: Controlled Assessment will guide you through the processes of research and investigation, development of ideas, planning, carrying out practical tasks and evaluating.

Unit 1 is divided into topics often with sub topics within the topic. Topics are set out in sections to help you work through the information. Each topic begins with learning objectives (**What will I learn?**) and includes an Assessment for Learning section (**Check your understanding**) so that you can test your knowledge and understanding. There are **activities** included to help assess your learning and in the Exam Practice feature there are **practice questions** for the theory examination. In addition there are tips to teach the skills you need to do well in the written examination to help you develop and achieve your potential.

Unit 2 will help you understand and apply your knowledge to the tasks chosen for Controlled Assessment. Two tasks have to be completed for Controlled Assessment. You will be given a set of tasks to choose from and your teacher will help you to choose the most suitable ones for you.

All sections of Controlled Assessment will have what is known as 'assessment criteria' which define what is being tested. The aim of Controlled Assessment is to enable you to apply knowledge gained from your lessons in a practical situation. There are examples of completed Controlled Assessment for Task 1 and Task 2, with detailed notes on the assessment criteria to guide you through the process and to help you to achieve the best results possible.

Home economics and food education are constantly changing as new guidelines and food laws are introduced. Manufacturers are introducing new products in line with healthy eating advice, eating habits and consumer demands.

We hope you enjoy the course and find it useful in developing your understanding of food and in improving your practical skills.

Good luck

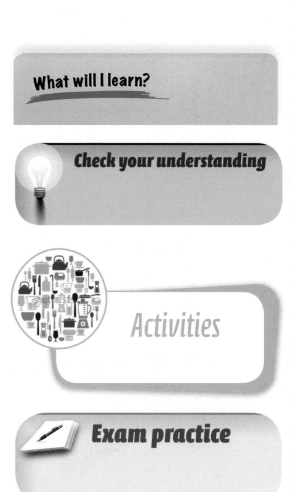

What will I learn?

Check your understanding

Activities

Exam practice

Topic 1: Nutrition, diet and health throughout life

What will I learn?

- The importance of healthy eating and a healthy diet.
- Nutrients and other substances in food that are important for growth and good health.
- Guidelines or advice given on how much of different foods we should be eating every day in order to grow properly and remain healthy.
- Possible consequences of not following guidelines and advice.

Nutrition, diet and health underpin the knowledge you will need to understand the subject.

1.1 Healthy eating

A **diet** is simply the food and drink that we take in every day. Everyone has a diet and some people follow a special diet such as a weight loss diet, a vegetarian diet, a low fat diet, a low salt diet or a high fibre diet. (See Topic 2 on Nutritional needs of individuals.)

Our diet should include a variety of foods, so that we get all the **nutrients** that we need.

A nutrient is the material in food needed for:

- Energy and warmth
- Building new body cells and repairing worn cells
- Keeping the body in a healthy condition
- Making the body work properly.

It is very important that we eat:

- The right amount of food for how active we are
- A variety of different foods.

This will give us a **healthy, balanced diet.** A healthy, balanced diet means eating a variety of different foods in the right amount for our particular needs. A healthy, balanced diet contains a variety of foods. We can think of foods belonging to one of five different groups:

- Bread, rice, potatoes, pasta and other starchy foods
- Fruit and vegetables
- Milk and dairy foods
- Meat, fish, poultry, eggs, beans, lentils and nuts
- Foods and drinks high in fat and/or sugar.

There are no unhealthy foods but there are unhealthy diets. An unhealthy diet is one that is high in fat, sugar and salt and low in dietary fibre.

As well as having the right balance of foods and drinks, it is also important to take in the right amount of **kilocalories** for you. We also use another unit of measurement called the kilojoule:

1 kilojoule (kJ) = 1,000 Joules (J)

1 kilocalorie (kcal) = 1,000 calories

1 kilocalorie (kcal) = 4.2 kilojoules (kJ)

In the UK, many children and adults are obese and this means that many people are consuming more kilocalories than they need. Research has shown that there are links between an unhealthy diet and obesity, high blood pressure, coronary heart disease, some types of cancer and tooth decay.

It is important to eat the right amount of food as well as a variety of food and drinks.

To help people choose a healthy, balanced diet, health experts and the government have put together some **dietary guidelines.** Dietary guidelines are advice or recommendations for a healthy diet.

To make these guidelines easier to follow, the **Food Standards Agency** has produced the **Eatwell plate.** These guidelines are for everyone over two years old who is in general good health**.**

Key terms

Nutrients – chemicals or substances found in food.

Kilocalories – a measurement of the energy value of foods.

Food Standards Agency – a UK government body that deals with food issues.

The Eatwell plate – a 'plate' diagram to show the amount of food we should be eating from each of the five sections.

The eatwell plate

food.gov.uk

Use the eatwell plate to help you get the balance right. It shows how much of what you eat should come from each food group.

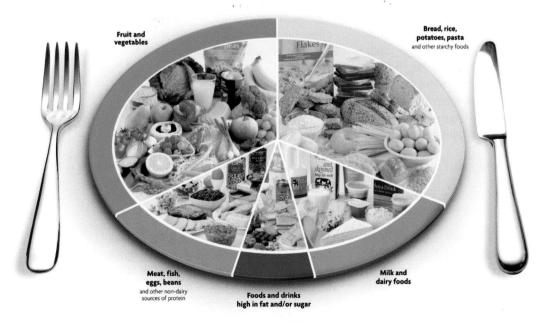

What do these guidelines mean?

Guidelines	What it means	Why?	How much?
1. Base your meals on starchy foods	This means that most of the food on our 'plate' should be a starchy food such as rice, pasta, bread, potato (but not chips), oats, cassava, quinoa or yam.	These foods will supply energy and will give us a variety of vitamins, minerals and fibre, especially if brown or wholemeal varieties are eaten.	Eat plenty, choose wholegrain varieties if you can.
2. Eat lots of fruit and vegetables	Fresh fruit and vegetables are excellent. Canned, frozen and dried varieties also provide nutrients. Fruit and vegetables juices also count.	These foods supply a variety of vitamins, minerals and fibre as well as **antioxidants**.	At least five **portions** a day.
3. Eat more fish	Eat a variety of fish, both fresh and canned. Avoid eating too much canned fish, which contains a lot of salt.	Oily fish contains **omega 3 fatty acids** which are important for a healthy heart. Fish contains vitamins, minerals as well as protein.	At least two portions a week, one of which should be oily fish.
4 (i) Cut down on saturated fat	Eat few foods that contain a lot of saturated fat such as butter, cooking oil, cheese, cream, pastries, cakes, biscuits.	Too much **saturated fat** is bad for our health.	Eat fewer high fat foods. Foods which have more than 5g saturates per 100g are considered to be high in fat.
4 (ii) Cut down on sugar	We eat too much sugar. There is a lot of '**hidden sugar**' in foods and drinks.	Too much sugar causes obesity and tooth decay and can contribute to type 2 diabetes.	50% of our daily energy should come from carbohydrates but only 11% of that should come from sugar.
5. Try to eat less salt	Cutting down on salt and being aware that some foods contain a lot of salt. Examples of foods high in salt are cheese, bacon, yeast extract, peanut butter, snack foods, some breakfast cereals, pizzas, cooked meat products, sauces and takeaway foods.	Too much salt has a bad effect on the body. The chemical name for salt is sodium chloride. It is the sodium part of salt that is bad. It can raise blood pressure and put extra strain on our kidneys.	Not more than 6g a day (a small teaspoonful). Babies and children should have less salt than adults.
6. Drink plenty of water	Many people do not drink enough water.	Water helps with digestion, removes waste, controls body temperature, helps concentration and prevents **dehydration**.	We need to drink 6–8 glasses a day.
7. Do not skip breakfast	**Breakfast** is the most important meal of the day. The body needs to have a good variety of nutrients and energy to set it up for the day.	Eating breakfast means we feel more alert, concentrate well and are less likely to eat high fat and sugary snacks mid-morning.	A variety of breakfast foods may be eaten. Many breakfast cereals are very high in sugar and salt, many are **fortified** with vitamins and minerals.
8. Get active and try to be a healthy weight	Doing regular exercise such as walking, dancing, cycling or sporting activity and keeping weight to your **BMI**.	It keeps us alert, makes us feel more confident and cuts down the risk of developing coronary heart disease and cancer.	30 minutes of moderate activity several times a week.

5 a day logo – we should eat at least 5 portions of fruit and vegetables a day.

What counts as a portion?

1 apple, banana, pear, orange, apricot, peach, nectarine

2 plums

1 medium tomato or 7 cherry tomatoes

½ grapefruit

1 large slice of melon or pineapple

3 heaped tablespoons of carrots or other vegetable, beans and pulses

3 heaped tablespoons of fruit salad or any canned or stewed fruit

1 heaped tablespoon of dried fruit

1 handful of grapes, cherries or berries

A dessert bowl of salad

A glass of fruit juice

Key terms

Antioxidants – substances found in vitamins A, C and E that are needed for good health and help protect the body against disease.

Portion – the size and weight of food we eat. A portion is about 80g in weight or 125 ml of juice.

Omega 3 – fatty acids that are important for a healthy heart.

Hidden sugar – sugar that you are not aware of in a product, often written on the ingredient list under chemical names such as glucose, glucose syrup, dextrose, lactose, fructose, sucrose, invert sugar, hydrolysed starch.

Saturated fat – a fat that comes from an animal source and can be bad for our health.

Dehydration – is when the body is short of water. Water is lost through sweat, urine, faeces and breathing and needs to be replaced.

Breakfast – breaking the 'fast'. Fasting is the period when we do not eat such as when we are sleeping.

Fortified – to have vitamins or minerals added.

BMI – body mass index, a measurement for body fat.

5 a day campaign – a government campaign to encourage us to eat at least 5 portions of fruit and vegetables a day.

Some meals or snacks are made up of food from more than one of the food groups on the Eatwell plate. These are called **combination** or **composite** foods.

Examples are cottage pie, pizzas, pasties, sandwiches, curry with rice. A good example of a combination or composite food is a beef lasagne.

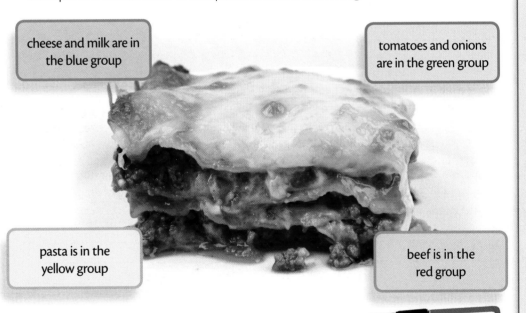

cheese and milk are in the blue group

tomatoes and onions are in the green group

pasta is in the yellow group

beef is in the red group

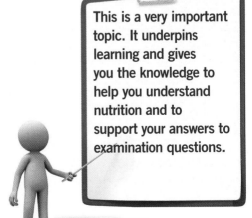

This is a very important topic. It underpins learning and gives you the knowledge to help you understand nutrition and to support your answers to examination questions.

Group	Examples	Colour code
1	Bread, other cereals, potatoes	Yellow
2	Fruit and vegetables	Green
3	Milk and dairy foods	Blue
4	Meat, fish, poultry, eggs, beans	Red
5	Food and drinks high in sugar and fat	Purple

Activities

1. Study the Eatwell plate. Why do you think the green and yellow sections are the largest sections and the purple section the smallest?

2. Plan a day's meals: breakfast, midday and evening meal including snacks and drinks.
   Show how your choice includes foods from the five food groups on the Eatwell plate

3. Carry out research on the amount of sugar in a range of foods and drinks. Record your findings under the headings:
   - name of food or drink
   - carbohydrates per 100g
   - of which sugars per 100g.

   Identify foods that have the highest amount of sugars per 100g.

Check your understanding

1. Give four examples of food from each of the five food groups on the Eatwell plate.

2. Use the foods listed on the chart to fill in the amount of fat and saturated fat they contain. You will find this information on any of the following:
   - food labels
   - pre-packaged samples of the foods
   - a nutritional analysis programme.

Name of food	Grams of fat in every 100g of the food	Grams of saturated fat in every 100g of the food
Baked beans in tomato sauce		
Wholemeal bread		
Minced beef		
Shredded wheat		
Canned sardines		
Plain yogurt		
Digestive biscuits		
Plain crisps		
Sausage roll		
Cheddar cheese		
Cottage cheese		
Cornish pasty		

a) List the five foods that have the highest fat content.
b) List the five foods that have the lowest fat content.
c) List the five foods that have the highest saturated fat content.
d) List the five foods that have the lowest saturated fat content.

3. A Hawaiian Pizza is made from a bread dough base and a tomato topping wiith ham, sweet corn, pineapple pieces, onion and cheese.

Complete the chart placing the ingredients in the correct group.

Group 1 – yellow	
Group 2 – green	
Group 3 – blue	
Group 4 – red	
Group 5 – purple	

1.2 Guidelines and understanding nutritional information

The **dietary guidelines** set out by the government help us to eat a healthy balanced diet. (See Topic 1.1 on page 8.)

Our energy and nutritional needs vary according to age, size, state of health and the physical activity we do. It simply means that we may, for various reasons, need more or less of a particular nutrient on a daily basis in order to remain healthy. This is known as our **nutritional requirement**. It varies between individuals and life stages.

Key terms

Dietary guidelines – advice on foods to eat in order to maintain health.

Nutritional requirements – estimates of energy and nutrients needed by individuals or groups of people.

Dietary reference values – estimates of the amounts of energy and nutrients needed daily.

The guidelines are based on advice given by health professionals, who have worked out how much of each nutrient our bodies need. This information is called the **dietary reference value** (DRVs). DRVs show the amount of energy and nutrients needed by groups of people for good health. The groups of people are based on age, gender (male or female) and for pregnant women and women who are breastfeeding.

DRVs are there to give people some idea of the amount of energy and nutrients that they need. They are very helpful for people who are providing foods in places such as hospitals, schools and residential homes because they have a duty to provide healthy, balanced meals to those people. DRVs do not apply to people who have a health condition or illness, as their needs for energy or particular nutrients may be different.

There are two types of estimate:

Reference nutrient intake (RNI) used for protein, vitamins and minerals.

Estimated average requirement (EAR) used for energy.

The amount of each nutrient we need is called the nutritional requirement.

There is also information on food labels called **guideline daily amounts** (GDAs). These were developed by food manufacturers to help people make a choice when buying food. GDAs give more detailed nutritional information on **kilocalories or kilojoules**, sugars, fat, saturates and salt. Each GDA is for an average adult.

The Food Standards Agency has also produced information which is aimed at helping people when buying foods. It is called the traffic light scheme, where the colours have the following information:

Red: the food is high in fat, salt or sugar.

Amber: the food has a medium level of fat, salt or sugar.

Green: the food is low in fat, salt or sugar.

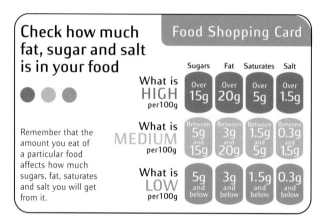

The Food Standards Agency traffic lights scheme on food labels

Guideline daily amounts are shown on food labels

Each serving contains

Calories	Sugars	Fat	Saturates	Salt
218	**6.3g**	**3.2g**	**1.4g**	**0.2g**
11%	7%	5%	7%	3%

of an adult's guideline daily amount

Estimated average requirements (EARs) for energy

Age	Males		Females	
	MJ/day	kcal/day	MJ/day	kcal/day
0–3 months	2.28	545	2.16	515
4–6 month	2.89	690	2.69	645
7–9 months	3.44	825	3.20	765
10–12 months	3.85	920	3.61	865
1–3 years	5.15	1 230	4.86	1 165
4–6 years	7.16	1 715	6.46	1 545
7–10 years	8.24	1 970	7.28	1 740
11–14 years	9.27	2 220	7.72	1 845
15–18 years	11.51	2 755	8.83	2 110
19–50 years	10.60	2 550	8.10	1 940
51–59 years	10.60	2 550	8.00	1 900
60–64 years	9.93	2 380	7.99	1 900
65–74 years	9.71	2 330	7.96	1 900
75+	8.77	2 100	7.61	1 810
Pregnancy			+0.8	+200
Lactation			+1.9	+450

Source – Department of Health Dietary Reference values for Food Energy and Nutrients for the United Kingdom London: HMSO, 1991

Reference nutrient intakes for vitamins

Age	Vitamin A µg/day	Thiamin Mg/day	Riboflavin Mg/day	Vitamin B$_{12}$ µg/day	Folate µg/day	Vitamin C Mg/day	Vitamin D µg/day
Children							
0–3 months	350	0.2	0.4	0.3	50	25	8.5
4–6 months	350	0.2	0.4	0.3	50	25	8.5
7–9 months	350	0.3	0.4	0.4	50	25	7
10–12 months	350	0.5	0.4	0.4	50	25	7
1–3 years	400	0.5	0.6	0.5	70	30	7
4–6 years	500	0.7	0.8	0.8	100	30	*
7–10 years	500	0.7	1.0	1.0	150	30	*
Males							
11–14 years	600	0.9	1.2	1.2	200	35	*
15–18 years	700	1.1	1.3	1.5	200	40	*
19–50 years	700	1.0	1.3	1.5	200	40	*
50+ years	700	0.9	1.3	1.5	200	40	*
Females							
11–14 years	600	0.7	1.1	1.2	200	35	*
15–18 years	600	0.8	1.1	1.5	200	40	*
19–50 years	600	0.8	1.1	1.5	200	40	*
50+ years	600	0.8	1.1	1.5	200	40	*
Pregnancy	+ extra 100	+ extra 0.1	+ extra 0.3	No increase	+ extra 100	+ extra 10	+ extra 10
Lactation	+ extra 350	+ extra 0.2	+ extra 0.5	+ extra 0.5	+ extra 60	+ extra 30	+ extra 10

Source – Department of Health Dietary Reference values for Food Energy and Nutrients for the United Kingdom London: HMSO, 1991

Reference nutrient intakes for minerals and protein

Age	Calcium mg/day	Sodium mg/day	Potassium mg/day	Iron mg/day	Protein g/day
Children					
0–3 months	525	210	800	1.7	12.5
4–6 months	525	280	850	4.3	12.7
7–9 months	525	320	700	7.8	13.7
10–12 months	525	350	700	7.8	14.9
1–3 years	350	500	800	6.9	14.5
4–6 years	450	700	1100	6.1	19.7
7–10 years	550	1200	2200	8.7	28.3

Age	Calcium mg/day	Sodium mg/day	Potassium mg/day	Iron mg/day	Protein g/day
Males					
11–14 years	1000	1600	3100	11.3	42.1
15–18 years	1000	1600	3500	11.3	55.2
19–50 years	700	1600	3500	8.7	55.5
50+ years	700	1600	3500	8.7	53.3
Females					
11–14 years	800	1600	3100	14.8	41.2
15–18 years	800	1600	3500	14.8	45.0
19–50 years	700	1600	3500	14.8	45.0
50+ years	700	1600	3500	8.7	46.5
Pregnancy	No increase	No increase	No increase	No increase	+ extra 6g
Lactation	550	No increase	No increase	No increase	+ extra 11g

Source – Department of Health Dietary Reference values for Food Energy and Nutrients for the United Kingdom London: HMSO, 1991

MJ – Megajoule = a unit of energy, mega (symbol M) = a factor of a million

mg – milligram = one thousandth of a gram: 1/1000g

µg – micromilligram = a millionth of a milligram: 1/1,000,000g

Key terms

Reference nutrient intake – the amount of protein, vitamins and minerals needed daily.

Estimated average requirement – the amount of energy needed by different groups of people.

Guideline daily amounts – the nutritional information found on food labels.

Kilocalories – a unit of energy; usually written in short as kcal.

Activity

1. a) How much vitamin B12 does a 13-year-old boy need?

   b) How much vitamin B12 does a 72-year-old man need?

   c) Can you explain why an elderly man needs more vitamin B12 than a teenage boy?

2. a) How much protein does a 17-year-old female need?

   b) How much protein does a 17-year-old male need?

   c) Can you explain why there is a difference in these figures?

Check your understanding

1. What is meant by the terms: DRV and RNI?

2. What is meant by guideline daily amounts? Give two reasons why this information may be useful.

1.3 Energy balance

Energy is needed by the body to stay alive. It gives us the ability to move around, stay warm and be active. It keeps the body working – heartbeat, breathing, digestion and sending messages to the brain. This amount is called **basal metabolic rate**. The basal metabolic rate is the rate at which a person uses energy to maintain the basic functions of the body.

Energy is provided by food and drink. It comes from the fat, carbohydrate, protein and alcohol in the diet. The amount of energy needed varies from one individual to another. The amount depends on factors such as age, state of health, physical activity levels and gender.

Age

Children need a lot of energy as they are usually active and are growing. Teenagers need more energy than adults because they are still growing. As people get older their energy needs are less; they have stopped growing but need some energy for activities.

State of health

Some illnesses may affect energy needs. The energy needs of a pregnant woman, for example, will increase to cope with the demands of the growing baby on her body.

Physical activity level

The more physically active you are, the more energy you will use. People who do work which uses up large amounts of energy such as building work, farming and forestry work should eat enough energy-giving foods regularly during the day. Different activities use different amounts of energy as shown below:

Activity	Kilocalories used in 20 minutes
Walking	99
Brisk walking	150
Mowing the lawn	165
Cycling	180
Aerobics	195
Tennis	240
Swimming (slow crawl)	195
Running	300
Cleaning and dusting	75

Gender

On average boys and men have slightly higher requirements than girls and women because they are generally bigger and have more muscle. However, everyone has individual needs so a tall, very active girl will use up more energy than a small non-active boy.

Energy measurement

Energy intake is often referred to by the metric measurement of kilojoules (kJ).

The most familiar unit of measurement is the kilocalorie (kcal), which is often written as Calorie (kcal). There are 1,000 calories in 1 kcal (or Calorie).

To convert kilocalories (kcal) to kilojoules (kJ):

1 kcal = 1000 calories = 4184 kJ

1MJ (megajoule) = 1,000,000 = 1 million joules

1 kJ (kilojoule) = 1000 = 1 thousand joules

Energy balance

To maintain body weight, it is necessary to balance the energy we take in from food and drink (**energy input**) with the energy we use in physical activity (**energy output**):

- If we take in the same amount of energy each day that we use for activities, our weight will stay the same and the balance will be correct.
- If we take in more energy each day than we use for activities, the body will store the excess as fat and we will gain weight.
- If we take in less energy each day than we use for activities, the body will draw on its store of fat and we will get thinner.

Striking the balance – the seesaw

■ EI = Energy Input

■ EO = Energy Output

weight maintenance
EI = EO

weight gain
EI > EO

weight loss
EI < EO

Where does the energy value of food come from?

The energy value of food comes from the macronutrients: fat, carbohydrates and protein.

- The best source is carbohydrate foods, starch and sugar.
- The most concentrated source is fat.
- The body prefers to use protein foods for growth and repair but will use it for energy if there is not enough carbohydrate and fat in the diet.

The energy values of the three macronutrients are shown below:

1 gram of pure carbohydrate = 4 kcal

1 gram of pure fat = 9 kcal

1 gram of pure protein = 4 kcal

Alcohol also provides the body with energy:

1 gram of pure alcohol = 29.4 kcal

Activities

1. Your friend is overweight and spends a lot of time watching television and playing computer games. Your friend needs to know what to do to lose weight.

   Give your friend advice.

2. Judy is a teenager who has taken up swimming and running. She does these every day for at least an hour. She has cut down on her food intake, and eats no sugary and fatty foods.

   Explain what is likely to happen to Judy's weight and give reasons.

Children and young people should be encouraged to have at least 60 minutes of moderate exercise such as walking, running, cycling, swimming every day to improve bone strength and to maintain a healthy bodyweight.

Check your understanding

1. Name three nutrients that are good sources of energy.

2. Explain what is meant by energy balance.

3. Suggest three factors that influence an individual's energy needs.

Stretch and challenge

1. Using nutritional analysis data or food labels, find out the energy value of a range of foods such as potato crisps, pies, salads, fruit, fish, cheese, pizza.

   Record your results in a chart and comment on your findings.

Name of food	kJ per 100 grams	Kcal per 100g
Example: milk chocolate	2177	520

2. Extend your knowledge on nutrition and healthy eating by collecting newspaper articles or email bulletins on current topics that are of interest to consumers.

1.4 Nutrients

This is a large topic so we will look at all the nutrient groups individually in the next few topics.

There are five main groups of nutrients. These five groups can be divided into two groups:

Macronutrients: these are needed by the body in large amounts. They are carbohydrates, protein and fat.

Micronutrients: these are needed by the body in small amounts. They are vitamins and minerals.

In addition to these nutrients, the body also needs water and fibre.

> This is a very important topic. It underpins learning and gives you the knowledge to help you understand nutrition and to support your answers to examination questions.

1.5 Proteins

Protein is a macronutrient.

Every cell in the body contains protein. Protein is needed by the body for growth, for the repair of body cells if they are damaged and for some energy. See the tables on pages 13 and 14 for amounts needed daily (reference nutrient intake).

Proteins are made up of simpler units called **amino acids**. There are twenty amino acids that make up a variety of proteins. When mixed together in different numbers and combinations they make different proteins.

Amino acids can be compared with different beads on a necklace. You can mix the beads together in any combination in the same way that combinations of amino acids form different proteins.

Of these 20 amino acids, 11 can be made by the body from the protein foods we eat. They are called non-essential amino acids. The other 9, called the **essential amino acids**, have to be provided ready made by the protein food we eat.

Essential amino acids have a **high biological value** and are found in animal foods such as meat, fish, poultry, milk and dairy products, cheese and eggs.

Non-essential amino acids have a **low biological value** and are found in plant foods such as rice, pasta, wheat, beans, pulses, nuts and seeds.

Soya beans are an exception as it is a plant food that contains all the essential amino acids.

Non-essential does not mean that the amino acids are not needed or used: it simply means that the food is missing in one or more of the essential amino acids. To make up for this loss we need to eat a mixture of protein foods. Vegetarians, in particular, have to rely on combining or mixing two protein foods to get all the essential amino acids. Examples are:

- Beans on toast
- Rice with dhal (lentils)
- Chick peas with couscous.

Combining two types of protein food is called the **complementation of protein**.

A vegan diet is made up entirely of plant foods such as beans, pulses, nuts, cereals, seeds, fruit, vegetables, soya milk and soya products. It is important that vegans eat a good mixture of plant proteins, especially soya products. (See Topic 2.7 on vegetarian diets.)

Everyone needs to have protein every day but the amount we need changes as we get older:

- Babies, children and teenagers need more protein than adults because their bodies are still growing.
- Adults need some protein to maintain and repair their bodies, for nail and hair growth and healing of wounds, for example.
- Pregnant and breastfeeding women need extra protein for the development of the baby.

Activity

These are daily protein requirements of individual groups.

Explain why a different amount of protein is needed by each group.

Age	RNI for protein
Male 15–50 years	55.5g
Female 15–50	45g
Pregnant women	51g
Breastfeeding (lactating) women	56g

Key terms

Amino acids – simpler units of protein, made up of long chains.

High biological value – protein foods containing all the essential amino acids.

Low biological value – protein foods lacking in one or more of the essential amino acids.

Check your understanding

1. Match the words to the description:

High biological value	must be provided ready made from a protein food.
Low biological value	a protein food that contains all the essential amino acids.
Essential amino acids	the mixing of two types of protein food to get the full range of amino acids.
Complementation of proteins	a protein food that does not contain the essential amino acids.

2. Name four foods that are good sources of high biological value protein.

3. Name four foods that are good sources of low biological value protein.

1.6 Carbohydrates

Carbohydrate is a macronutrient.

Plant food is the most important source of carbohydrate. Carbohydrate is changed to glucose during the process of digestion. Glucose is used to provide us with energy.

There are two main types of carbohydrate:

- starch
- sugars.

Examples of starchy and sugary foods

Key terms

Dietary fibre – the edible part of a plant which cannot be broken down during digestion.

Polysaccharide – a complex carbohydrate, poly = many, saccharide = sugar.

Starch is a more complex carbohydrate, made up of long chains (molecules). Starch is the main store of energy for plants. It is broken down during digestion to glucose units and used for energy in the body. Every function of the body – movement, digestion of food, growth – needs a constant supply of energy to make it happen.

Dietary fibre or non-starch **polysaccharide** is the part of the plant that gives strength and structure. It cannot be digested by the body but is important in the diet for helping the body get rid of waste and keeping our bowels healthy.

Adults should have at least 18g of fibre a day. A high fibre diet helps to prevent bowel disorders such as cancer and helps to reduce cholesterol levels in the body.

Starchy foods that are especially high in dietary fibre are wholemeal bread, beans, lentils, wholemeal pasta, wholemeal flour and breakfast cereals that contain bran and oats.

Starchy foods provide other important nutrients as well as starch and dietary fibre. Bread contains protein, B vitamins and calcium. Rice and pasta are both high in protein and low in fat. Pulses such as beans and lentils are excellent for protein and vitamin A.

We should eat a lot of starchy, fibre-rich foods and cut down on our sugary foods. Half of our energy from food every day should come from starchy foods. They add bulk to the diet and help to fill us up so we are less likely to eat fatty and sugary snacks.

Sugars

Examples of sugars are sucrose (sugar we use in drinks and other foods), fructose (the sugar in fruit), glucose, lactose (the sugar in milk) and maltose.

Sugar group	Name of sugar	Examples of foods containing the sugar
Simple sugars or monosaccharides	Fructose	Fruits, fruit juice, honey
	Glucose	Sugar used in drinks and cooking
	Galactose	Milk
Double sugars or disaccharides	Sucrose	Granulated sugar, caster sugar, brown sugars which are used to sweeten drinks and used in cakes, biscuit and puddings; these come from either sugar cane or sugar beet
	Lactose	Milk and some dairy products such as yogurt
	Maltose	Barley, and added as malt to some types of malted biscuits and drinks

Different types of sucrose (double sugars)

We also use sugar in drinks and in biscuits, cakes and puddings to sweeten and improve texture. This type of sugar provides empty calories – it supplies us with energy but has no extra nutrients.

Many food products such as soups, sauces and breakfast cereals contain 'hidden sugar' because we do not always realise that it is in the food.

Research shows that sugar encourages tooth decay. To prevent tooth decay, we should cut down on sticky, sugary foods and drinks, especially between meals.

Change4life is a campaign to help us eat more healthily and be more active.

There are many ways of cutting down on sugar intake:

- Choose lower in sugar options or those foods labelled as 'reduced sugar'.
- Choose fruit instead of sugary snacks.
- Choose sugar-free drinks and foods. Many of these have an artificial sweetener added instead of sugar.
- Use an artificial sweetener to sweeten instead of sugar.

The Eatwell plate (Topic 1.1 on page 7) shows how much carbohydrate we should have compared with other foods.

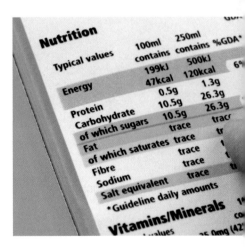

Read nutrition labels to find out how much sugar the food contains

Too much carbohydrate food

If we eat too much carbohydrate and do not use up the energy we have consumed in food, the body will store the excess energy from the carbohydrate as fat under the skin.

Too little carbohydrate food

If we do not eat enough carbohydrate food, our bodies will use fat and protein foods to provide energy. The body will use the fat stored as body fat and we will get thinner.

Glycaemic Index (GI) is a measure of the effects of carbohydrates on blood glucose (sugar) levels. Carbohydrates break down during digestion and release glucose into the blood stream.

Some carbohydrates break down quickly during digestion and release glucose quickly into the blood stream. These have a high GI. Examples of foods high in GI are potatoes, croissants, cornflakes, white bread.

Some carbohydrate foods break down slowly, releasing glucose gradually into the bloodstream. These have a low GI. Foods with a low GI have health benefits. Eating foods low in GI during the day can provide lasting energy. Examples of foods low in GI are most fruit and vegetables, wholegrain bread, pasta, beans, lentils and milk.

Examples of lower-sugar foods; reduced amounts of sugar, sugar-free, with a lower sugar option

Activities

1. Visit the Change4life website and make a list of suggestions for sugar swaps.

2. Read the ingredients list on the food label:

   Ingredients: maize, sugar, peanuts, honey, barley malt flavouring, molasses, salt.

   a) Identify names of sugars and ingredients that contain starch.

   b) Guess the food.

Check your understanding

1. Give one reason why our bodies need carbohydrate foods.

2. Why should we eat more starchy foods than sugary foods?

3. Suggest four ways of cutting down on the sugar you eat.

4. List three foods that are high in fibre.

Topic 1: Nutrition, diet and health
throughout life
Fats and oils

1.7 Fats and oils

Fat is a macronutrient.

Fats can either be hard fats, which are solid at room temperature or fats which are liquid at room temperature known as oils. When oil hardens, it becomes solid.

The chemical name for a fat molecule is a triglyceride. Triglycerides are one part glycerol and three parts fatty acids. A fatty acid can either be **saturated** or **unsaturated**.

It is possible to make a solid fat from liquid by adding hydrogen. This is known as hydrogenation. These fats are known as hydrogenated vegetable oils or trans fats.

Research has shown that hydrogenated vegetable oils or trans fats can be bad for the body, leading to health problems such as heart disease, obesity and bone disorders.

Hydrogenated fats and oils are widely used in bakery products, by restaurants and in takeaway food.

Saturated fatty acids	Unsaturated fatty acids
saturated fatty acid	*unsaturated fatty acid*
The carbon atoms are linked to hydrogen atoms.	The carbon atoms are not full up with hydrogen atoms.
The carbon atoms cannot take on any more hydrogen atoms.	The carbon atoms could take on more hydrogen atoms.
	The carbon atoms form double bonds.
They are saturated.	They are unsaturated.
Solid fats are mostly made up of saturated fatty acids. Examples are butter, lard, suet, block margarine, fat on meat.	One double bond means that the fat is a mono-unsaturated fatty acid.
	An example is olive oil.
There is a high amount of **cholesterol** in saturated fats.	More than one double bond and the fat is a poly-unsaturated fatty acid. Examples are sunflower oil, rapeseed oil, nut oil, corn oil.
	The amount of cholesterol is lower in unsaturated fats, especially polyunsaturated fats.

Fats and oils provide a very concentrated source of energy and essential fatty acids such as omega 3 and omega 6.

Fats and oils also carry important **fat-soluble vitamins**.

Omega 3 and omega 6 fatty acids have health benefits. They are known to help prevent coronary heart disease and prevent joint diseases.

Foods rich in omega 3 include fish oils such as salmon, sardines and mackerel. Foods rich in omega 6 include sunflower oil, flaxseed and soya oil.

Vitamin A and D are added by law to margarine. This is known as fortification.

Fat can be stored under the skin, and helps to keep us warm by insulating the body. All fats provide 9 kilocalories per gram. Too much fat in the diet can make us put on extra weight.

Saturated fats come mainly from animal sources. Examples are butter, cream and the fat on meat.

Unsaturated fats come mainly from plants and have health benefits.

How much fat do we need?

Fats should make up a very small part of our everyday meals and snacks. The Eatwell plate shows clearly how much we should have in comparison with the other four groups of food. Eating too many fatty foods can have a bad effect on health; it can increase the risk of illnesses such as heart disease.

The amount of fat in food varies. We can actually see fats and oils in the form of foods such as butter, lard, suet, margarine and spreads. We can also see fat on foods such as meat, for example a pork chop with a wide strip of white fat at the edge or the fatty part of bacon. When cheese melts on a pizza, we often see the fat as runny oil. The amount of fat in these examples of **visible fat** varies.

Here are some examples of typical fat and saturated fat content in visible fats and oils:

100g or (100 ml liquid) food	Fat in grams	Saturated fat in grams
Butter	82.9	49.3
Olive oil spread	59	14
Lard	100	44
Block margarine	75	25.7
Sunflower oil	92	11
Olive oil	91	14.3
White vegetable fat	100	34
Flora light spread	38	9.3

Many foods contain **invisible** or **hidden fat**. The amount of fat is shown on food labels. (See page 96 on food labelling.)

- Some foods such as cheese, cream, and sausages are fatty by nature.
- Some ready-made foods such as cakes, pastries, biscuits, ready meals, take-away foods, pizzas, snack foods have a very high fat content.
- Some foods such as doughnuts, chips, crisps are cooked in fat or oil, which adds to the fat content.

There are many ways in which we can cut down the amount of fat we eat. These are some examples:

- Use lower in fat options – choose low fat or reduced fat options of foods such as spreads, milk, cheese, biscuits and mayonnaise.
- Use less butter or margarine by spreading a thinner layer on bread and toast.
- Cut down on fatty food by eating fewer chips, pastry foods, biscuits and fatty snacks.
- Choose lean meats such as chicken or cut off the fat on meat, bacon and ham.
- Use a method of cooking such as grilling, microwaving, oven baking, steaming which uses less or no fat or oil.
- Dry fry mince and pour away the fat. Spoon off the fat from gravies and home-made soups.
- Check on the label for the fat content of foods such as minced beef and try to buy minced beef with no more than 5% fat content.

Cutting down on fat in the diet

Choose lower fat options

Choose foods containing less fat   *Choose methods of cooking which do not use extra oil or fat*

Fats are essential for correct growth and functioning of the body and for warmth.

If we do not have enough fat from the food we eat, we may not get enough energy from our food and we may become underweight; the growth of babies and young children will also be affected.

If we have too much fat from the food we eat and do not use up the energy, we will put on weight. Putting on extra weight will increase the risk of developing heart disease, which is a major cause of death in the UK. To reduce this risk we should eat less fatty food and increase the amount of fibre-rich food such as fruit, vegetables and wholegrain cereals. Regular exercise can help too.

Activities

1. Why do you think there is so much concern about:

   a) The type of fat we eat?

   b) The amount of fat we eat?

Key terms

Cholesterol – a fatty substance found in our blood and the food we eat.

Fat-soluble vitamins – vitamins A, D, E and K. These vitamins dissolve in fat.

Visible fat – fat or oil that we can actually see.

Hidden or invisible fat – the fat or oil that we cannot see in food products.

2. Match the following term to the description:

Saturated   Hydrogenated   Unsaturated   Fatty acid

Term	Description
	A chemical name for a fat molecule
	A process which turns liquid into solid fat
	The carbon atoms cannot take on any more hydrogen atoms
	The carbon atoms could take on more hydrogen atoms

3. Potatoes can be cooked using different methods of cooking. Using the table below name methods of cooking where:

   a) No fat or oil is added to the potato.

   b) Some fat or oil is added to the potato.

Name of method	
Cooking method where no fat or oil is added	
Cooking methods where fat or oil is added	

Check your understanding

1. Give three reasons why your body needs fat.

2. What is the difference between fats and oils?

3. Describe the difference between a saturated fat and an unsaturated fat.

4. Name three examples of a saturated fat.

5. Name three examples of an unsaturated fat.

Key terms

Water soluble – dissolves in water.

Fat soluble – dissolves in fat.

Remember

- Function = job or use in the body
- Sources = foods found in
- Deficiency = shortage or lack of

1.8 Vitamins

Vitamins are micronutrients.

Vitamins have different jobs to do in the body and are needed in small amounts. Vitamins can be divided into **water soluble** or **fat soluble**.

It is important to remember that:

- Each vitamin is known by its letter and by its chemical name.

- Each vitamin has a job (function) in the body.

- Each vitamin can be found in a particular food.

- The body can develop a deficiency if it does not have enough of a particular vitamin.

- Some vitamins may be lost during cooking.

Water-soluble vitamins

These are the vitamins in the B group, and vitamin C.

Good sources of the B group of vitamins

Vitamin B1

Chemical name: Thiamin.

Functions:

- Helps in the release of energy from carbohydrate foods.
- Helps the body to grow.
- Helps the nervous system to work properly.

Sources: red meat, liver, wholegrain cereals, yeast and yeast extract (Marmite), milk and dairy foods, eggs, seeds, nuts and beans.

Deficiency: a muscle wastage disease called beri-beri in countries where the diet is based on white rice.

Effect of cooking: destroyed by heat when cooking.

Vitamin B2

Chemical name: Riboflavin.

Functions:

- Helps in the release of energy from carbohydrate foods.
- Needed for growth in children.

Sources: red meat, liver, wholegrain cereals, yeast and yeast extract (Marmite), milk and dairy foods, eggs, seeds, nuts and beans.

Deficiency: can lead to dry skin and cracks around the mouth and nose.

Effect of cooking: none.

27

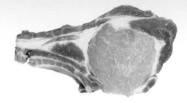

Vitamin B3

Chemical name: Niacin.

Functions:

- Helps in the release of energy from carbohydrate foods.
- Helps to lower levels of fat in the blood.

Sources: red meat, liver, wholegrain cereals, yeast and yeast extract (Marmite), milk and dairy foods, eggs, seeds, nuts and beans.

Deficiency: a disease called pellagra. Symptoms of pellagra are diarrhoea, a rough sore skin and confusion or memory loss.

Effect of cooking: none.

Vitamin B6

Chemical name: Pyrodoxin.

Function: helps the body use protein, carbohydrates and fat for different jobs.

Sources: red meat, liver, wholegrain cereals, yeast and yeast extract (Marmite), milk and dairy foods, eggs, seeds, nuts and beans.

Deficiency: **anaemia**, headaches, general weakness.

Effect of cooking: can be destroyed during cooking.

Vitamin B9

Chemical name: Folate.

Functions:

- Helps the body to use protein.
- Helps to form blood cells.

Sources: green leafy vegetables such as spinach, liver, potatoes, beans, seeds, wholegrain cereals, nuts, oranges and berry fruits.

Deficiency: a type of anaemia called megaloblastic anaemia, feeling sick with loss of appetite and diarrhoea. A chemical form called folic acid is given to pregnant women to help prevent a deformity in the baby called spina bifida.

Effect of cooking: **destroyed when food is kept hot for long periods.**

Key terms

Anaemia – a disease which can develop from low stores of iron in the body.

Collagen – the protein in connective tissue, a substance which binds cells together.

Antioxidant – helps to protect the body from chemicals from the air, water or food that could do harm.

Beta carotene – is changed to retinol in the body.

Vitamin B12

Chemical name: Cobalamin.

Functions:

- Helps the nervous system work properly.
- Helps in the production of red blood cells.

Sources: meat, milk, dairy foods.

Deficiency: a type of anaemia called pernicious anaemia. Vegans need to make sure they take supplements.

Effect of cooking: none.

Vitamin C

Chemical name: Ascorbic acid.

Functions:

- Helps the body absorb iron from food.
- Helps make **collagen** in the body.
- Acts as an **antioxidant**.

Sources: fruit and vegetables, especially citrus fruit, blackcurrants, kiwi fruit, potatoes, dark green vegetables such as broccoli, green peppers, Brussels sprouts.

Deficiency: anaemia if the body cannot absorb the iron in food, a disease called scurvy which gives rise to bleeding gums, tiredness and poor healing of wounds.

Effect of cooking: easily destroyed by heat and leaving food such as green vegetables exposed to oxygen in the air.

When preparing and cooking vitamin C rich fruit and vegetables it is important to:

- Buy as fresh as possible.
- Prepare just before using or cooking so as not leave exposed to oxygen in the air.
- Cook quickly in small amount of boiling water.
- Use any cooking liquid for sauce, gravy, stock.
- Serve straight away, do not keep hot.
- Consider using a method of cooking such as steaming or microwaving which does not need any water.

Good sources of vitamin C

Fat-soluble vitamins

Good sources of vitamin A

Vitamin A

Chemical name: Retinol.

Functions:

- Helps growth in children.
- Needed for night vision (ability to see shadows in the dark).
- Helps keep the lining of the throat, digestive system and lungs healthy.
- Acts as an antioxidant.

Sources: milk and dairy foods, oily fish and liver. It is added to margarine and spreads during manufacture. It is also found as **beta carotene** in plant foods such as green leafy vegetables, tomato, carrots, oranges, red peppers and spinach.

Deficiency: growth can be affected if we do not have enough, difficulty in seeing in the dark and difficulty in fighting off infections.

It is possible to have too much vitamin A in the diet. Vitamin A supplements should only be taken on the advice of a doctor.

Effect of cooking: none.

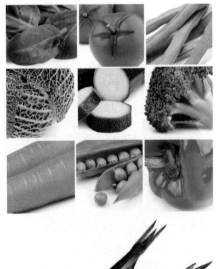

Good source of vitamin D

Key terms

Peak bone mass – when the bones have most minerals in them and are at their hardest.

Rickets – a bone disease in children when the bones become deformed.

Osteomalacia – means 'bad' bones.

Good sources of vitamin E

Good sources of vitamin K

Vitamin D

Chemical name: Cholecalciferol.

Functions:

- Helps to form strong bones and teeth especially during childhood and adolescence when it is important that bones reach their '**peak bone mass**'.
- Helps control the amount of calcium absorbed from food.

Sources: a little in liver, oily fish, milk and dairy foods. Most of our supply comes from sunlight when it is made under the skin and stored in the liver.

Deficiency: if there is a shortage of vitamin D, the calcium cannot be absorbed and the teeth and bones can become weak. This can lead to **rickets** and **osteomalacia**.

Effect of cooking: none.

Vitamin E

Chemical name: Tocopherol.

Functions:

- It acts as an antioxidant which helps protect the body from diseases.
- Evidence shows that it protects the body from certain types of cancer and heart disease.
- It protects the lining of the throat, lungs and digestive system.

Sources: nuts, seeds, wheatgerm oil, milk, egg yolk, polyunsaturated spreads and oils.

Deficiency: very rare.

Effect of cooking: none.

Vitamin K

Chemical name: none.

Functions:

- Helps blood clot.
- Helps to keep bones healthy.

Sources: green leafy vegetables, liver, bacon, cereals.

Deficiency: very rare.

Effect of cooking: none.

Activities

1. Using the information on the B group of vitamins, find examples of foods which are named as good sources of most of these vitamins.
2. Why do you think vitamin A and D are added to margarine and spreads?

Check your understanding

1. a) Name the water-soluble vitamins.

   b) Name the fat-soluble vitamins.

2. Give two functions for each of the vitamins named.

3. Give two food sources for each of the vitamins named.

4. Match the following deficiency diseases:

Shortage of iron and vitamin C in the diet	Shortage of vitamin A

Shortage of vitamin D and calcium in the diet

Shortage of riboflavin	Shortage of thiamine

anaemia	night blindness (difficulty seeing in the dark)
pellagra	dry skin, cracks in the skin around the mouth and nose

rickets

1.9 Minerals

Minerals are micronutrients.

These are needed in small amounts to carry out a variety of jobs in the body. Essential minerals include calcium, iron, magnesium, phosphorus, potassium, sodium, chlorine, selenium and zinc. They are needed in amounts of between 1mg and 100mg a day. Other minerals, known as trace minerals, are needed in very small amounts of less than 1mg a day. Examples are fluoride and iodine.

You need to know about nine minerals: calcium, fluoride, iron, magnesium, phosphorus, potassium, selenium, sodium and zinc.

Remember that:

- Each mineral has a job (function) in the body.
- Each mineral can be found in a food.
- A deficiency can develop if the body does not have enough of a particular mineral.

Remember

- Function = job or use in the body
- Sources = foods found in
- Deficiency = shortage or lack of

Calcium

Functions:

- Makes bones and teeth hard and strong.
- Helps blood to clot.
- Keeps nerves and muscles working properly.
- Helps with normal growth in children.

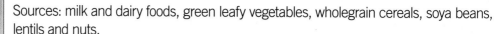

Sources: milk and dairy foods, green leafy vegetables, wholegrain cereals, soya beans, lentils and nuts.

- There are things that help calcium to be absorbed by the body to carry out its functions. Two examples are vitamin D rich foods and exercise.
- There are things that prevent calcium from being absorbed by the body to carry out its functions. Two examples are an acid found in wholegrain cereals called phytic acid and an acid found in spinach called oxalic acid.

Deficiency: rickets in children, a disease where the bones and teeth do not form properly. Adults can suffer from osteomalacia.

Vitamin D rich foods and sunlight are needed with calcium rich foods to enable the calcium to be absorbed by the body.

Bones should reach 'peak bone mass' during **adolescence**. Both calcium and vitamin D are needed for this to happen. Physical activity and exercise, such as running or walking, also help the bones to take in the calcium from food.

Key terms

Adolescence – the period during which a person develops from a child to an adult.

Haemoglobin – a red coloured protein in the blood.

Fluoride

Functions: helps to harden tooth enamel and prevent tooth decay.

Sources: tea and sea fish. It is added to drinking water in some areas.

Deficiency: teeth may be likely to develop decay. Too much fluoride can cause discolouration of the teeth.

Iron

Functions: helps to make **haemoglobin** in the red blood cells which carry oxygen to the body cells.

Sources: There are two types of iron:

- Haem iron, which is easily absorbed by the body, and is found in red meat, liver, corned beef.
- Non-haem iron, which is less easily absorbed and is found in wholegrain cereals, green leafy vegetables, beans, nuts, dried fruit and fortified breakfast cereals.

Vitamin C rich foods need to be eaten with iron rich foods to help the body absorb the iron.

- There are things that help iron to be absorbed by the body to carry out its functions. One example is to eat a vitamin C rich food at the same time as an iron rich food.
- There are things that prevent iron from being absorbed by the body to carry out its functions. Two examples are an acid found in wholegrain cereals called phytic acid and an acid found in spinach called oxalic acid.

Deficiency: anaemia (symptoms include tiredness, weakness, lack of energy, pale complexion). Adolescent girls need extra supplies of iron to replace the loss during their monthly periods. Pregnant women must have enough iron in their diet to supply their own body as well as the baby's store of iron.

healthy heart

A good supply of foods rich in calcium and iron will help towards strong bones and healthy blood.

Magnesium

Functions:

- Helps the bones to develop.
- Helps the nervous system to work properly.

Sources: green vegetables, meat, wholegrain cereals, nuts and seeds.

Deficiency: may cause high blood pressure and heart disease.

Phosphorus

Functions: essential for healthy bones and teeth and works with calcium.

Sources: a wide range of animal and plant foods.

Deficiency: none because it is found in so many foods.

Potassium

Functions:

- Helps to balance body fluids.
- Helps to lower blood pressure.
- Needed to keep the muscles of the heart healthy.

Sources: fruit and vegetables, coffee, potatoes and salt substitutes.

Deficiency: none.

Selenium

Functions:

- An antioxidant.
- Helps to protect against heart disease.

Sources: red meat, fish, cereals and Brazil nuts.

Deficiency: none.

Sodium

Functions:

- Helps to control the amount of water in the body.
- Helps the body to use energy.
- Helps to control the nerves and muscles.

Sources: salt, many processed foods such as snacks, ready meals, tinned and dried soups, takeaway food, bacon, ham, yeast extract and bought cakes and biscuits.

Deficiency: muscle cramps.

Too much sodium can lead to high blood pressure which puts strain on the heart. Too much sodium can also damage the kidneys.

Ways to cut down on salt:

- Cook with less salt. Use herbs, spices, lemon juice to flavour food instead.
- Check the label for the amount of salt in the food.

- Choose 'low salt' alternatives.
- Eat fewer salty meat products such as beefburgers, sausages and pies.
- Eat fewer processed foods and ready meals.

Zinc

Functions:

- Helps the immune system to fight disease and infections.
- Helps to heal wounds.

Sources: meat, dairy foods, pulses and wholegrain cereals.

Deficiency: evidence shows that it can lead to poor growth in children.

Nutrition label for a sweet and sour pork ready meal

Typical Values	Per 100g (as sold)	Per Pack (as consumed)	Guideline Daily Amount (GDA)*
Energy	470kJ 111kcal	1542kJ 364kcal	2000kcal
Protein	4.3g	14.2g	
Carbohydrate	21.9g	71.0g	
(of which sugars)	6.4g	20.7g	90g
Fat	0.5g	2.1g	70g
(of which saturates)	0.1g	0.3g	20g
Fibre	0.7g	2.1g	
Sodium	0.12g	0.41g	
(Equivalent as salt)	0.3g	1.0g	6g

Per pack microwaved provides

Calories	Sugar	Fat	Saturates	Salt	
364	20.7g	2.1g	0.3g	1.0g	* % of an average adults guideline daily amount.
18%	23%	3%	2%	17%	

High in salt

 Activities

1. Plan the following meals using good combinations of an iron rich and a vitamin C rich food. Identify the iron and the vitamin C foods each time.

   a) Breakfast

   b) Snack meal

   c) Main meal.

2. Collect labels of the foods listed under Sodium: sources on page 33.

   Find out how much 'salt of which sodium' per 100g they contain.

   Record your results in a chart and write a comment on your findings.

Check your understanding

1. What is the function of:

   a) Calcium?

   b) Iron?

2. Name two things that help with the absorption of calcium.

3. Name three foods which have salt added to them when they are made.

4. Why is it not good for the body to have too much sodium?

1.10 Dietary fibre

Dietary fibre is not classed as a nutrient but is needed for digestion. Dietary fibre or just 'fibre' is also called non-starch polysaccharide (NSP). (See Topic 1.6 Carbohydrates.)

The body needs fibre to help get rid of solid waste material (faeces). It does this by absorbing water, making the faeces soft and bulky so that it can pass easily along the intestines and out of the body. During this process all the waste is taken out of the body.

A diet rich in fibre makes us 'feel full' after a meal and stops us from feeling hungry for a long time. It helps to lower the amount of cholesterol in the blood. Fibre also helps to prevent constipation and lowers the risk of developing cancers of the intestines, especially in the bowel. A diet high in fibre is usually low in fat and is generally a healthy diet. Foods labelled as 'high in fibre' on the label must contain 6g fibre per 100g food.

We need fibre in our diet every day. Dietary guidelines recommend that we have at least 18g a day. Small children need less fibre than adults because of their smaller body size.

Fibre is found in leaves, leaf stalks, skins of fruit and vegetables and the outside skin on beans, nuts and seeds. It forms the stringy bits in plants such as celery and cabbage.

Good sources of fibre are: wholegrain rice, wholemeal, granary or seeded bread, wholemeal pasta, wholemeal flour, dried fruits, fresh fruit and vegetables (especially when the skin is eaten), nuts, beans, lentils, all varieties of seeds and wholegrain breakfast cereals such as Shredded wheat, bran flakes, porridge oats.

There are many ways of increasing the amount of fibre we eat:

- Choose wholegrain or wholemeal varieties of bread, rice and pasta.
- Add bran to other breakfast cereals.
- Add beans, peas or lentils to casseroles, curries and stews.
- Eat dried fruit or nuts instead of sugary and fatty snacks.
- Leave the skins and peel on fruit and vegetables whenever possible.
- Add chopped fresh or stewed fruit to breakfast cereals.

Remember, the more natural the food, the more fibre it will have.

Activities

1. List other ways of adding more fibre to the diet when making meals at home and in drinks and snacks.

2. Suggest ways of increasing the fibre content of a recipe for an apple crumble made from white flour, butter, sugar, peeled apples.

3. Compare the amount of fibre per serving in different breakfast cereals such as cornflakes, chocolate coated rice cereal, puffed wheat cereal, muesli, porridge oats, shredded wheat and a fruit and fibre cereal.

   Record your results in a chart and make a comment on your findings.

Check your understanding

1. Describe what fibre is.
2. Why does the body need fibre?
3. Name four foods that are good sources of fibre.

1.11 Water

Water is not a nutrient but is essential for life.

Our bodies are made up of about 60% water. Water has many functions in the body. It helps:

- To make up body cells and tissue.
- To make up body fluids such as blood, sweat, saliva, urine.
- Absorb nutrients.
- To keep the skin moist and healthy.
- To control body temperature.
- To keep the body hydrated.
- Concentration.

Water is lost from the body through sweat, urine, breathing and the faeces. This water has to be replaced by drinking water and other drinks and from eating watery foods.

We need to drink about 2 litres of water a day. This is roughly 6–8 glasses. More water is needed when we are in a hot climate or when doing physical activities or exercise.

A lack of water in the body leads to **dehydration**. These are some of the symptoms of dehydration:

- Headache
- Feeling weak

Key term

Dehydration – when the body is short of water.

- Very dark, concentrated urine
- Confusion
- Changes in blood pressure.

Water contains no energy.

Activity

Explain why drinking water is better than drinking lots of sweet, fizzy drinks.

Check your understanding

1. Give three functions of water in the body.
2. Explain what is meant by dehydration.

Exam practice

1. You have been asked to write a leaflet giving advice on how to promote and maintain a healthy lifestyle. Discuss the information you would include in the leaflet. [8]

2. Children's lunch boxes often contain foods high in fat and sugar.

   a) Suggest a suitable packed lunch for a six year old. [4]

   b) Discuss the health benefits of reducing the amount of foods high in fat and sugar in a child's diet. [6]

3. Different proteins 'complement' each other. Explain why it can be beneficial to include a mixture of protein foods in the diet. [6]

4. Some children are very active.

   a) Explain what happens if a child's intake of food and the energy used do not balance. [4]

   b) Discuss how a parent could provide a child with a healthy, balanced diet and healthy lifestyle. [6]

5. a) Explain what is meant by 'energy balance'. [2]

   a) Suggest ways of encouraging children to eat a healthy diet. [6]

6. Assess the importance of vitamins A, C, and E in the diet. [9]

7. Some fat is needed in the diet to maintain health. Explain the role of fat in the diet. [6]

Topic 2: Nutritional needs of individuals

2.1 Babies and pre-school children

Babies

Newborn babies should only have milk for the first four to six months of their life. After four to six months, small amounts of very soft foods are given to the baby as well as milk. This is called **'weaning'**. Weaning starts when the baby is showing signs that they are not satisfied on just a milk feed.

Department of Health guidelines are that babies are introduced to solid food from 26 weeks (6 months). By this time, the supply of iron the baby was born with will be starting to run out, so iron will need to be provided by the baby's diet.

Different and larger amounts of raw and cooked foods must be introduced to the baby very gradually because the baby has to get used to new tastes and textures as well as learning to swallow new foods. Foods to try first are:

- Baby rice mixed with the baby's usual milk.
- Pureed fruit and vegetables.

From 7 to 9 months, the range of foods being offered can be increased, although the food must still be pureed at first, progressing to mashed, as the baby gets used to more variety. Foods to try:

- A wider selection of fruit and vegetables.
- Beans, lentils chicken and fish (no bones).
- Well-cooked egg yolk.

From about 9 months onwards lumpier foods can be introduced as the baby will be able to cope with chewing and swallowing. Finger foods (e.g. breadsticks, slices of fruit and vegetables) can also be given to encourage the baby to be independent. Foods to try:

- Foods with more lumps.

Key term

Weaning – the gradual introduction of solid foods into the baby's diet.

- Cheese and yogurt.
- Pasta.
- Bread.

Foods to avoid:

- Some foods should be avoided during weaning because they may cause harm to the baby or because they are not needed in a healthy diet.
- Salt should not be added because the baby's kidneys cannot get rid of it.
- Sugar can cause tooth decay and babies can start to develop a preference for sweet foods.
- The baby could choke on whole nuts, so nuts must be chopped.
- Fatty and fried foods are difficult for the baby to digest and are not needed in the diet.
- Cows' milk can be given as a drink from 12 months. Before then, cows' milk can be used in small quantities mixed with other food, but breast milk or formula milk should be given as a drink.

In order to make the process of weaning go smoothly, parents should try to make mealtimes an enjoyable experience, without worrying about the mess. If the baby is able to enjoy touching the food and attempts to feed themselves, they are more likely to try different foods. Plenty of time for eating is needed, especially at first. Rushing or forcing the baby could lead to problems later on, so it is best to go at the baby's pace and stop when they have had enough.

Hot food must be cooled and tested before giving it to the baby and the baby should never be left unsupervised when eating in case they choke.

There is a wide range of commercially prepared baby foods suitable for weaning when parents are unable to make their own food. These are quick, easy to use, and convenient when away from the home. The ingredients and nutritional value are clearly labelled, so parents know what they are giving to the baby. However, these foods are more expensive than homemade versions and there may be wastage if the baby only has a small amount.

Activities

1. Try a range of baby food for different ages and comment on the flavour and texture.

2. Design a new recipe for a savoury or sweet baby food. Draw the packaging, including all the information someone purchasing the food would want to know.

Check your understanding

1. There are some foods that should not be given during weaning. Identify these foods and explain why they are not suitable.

2. Compare the advantages and disadvantages of homemade and commercially prepared baby food.

Young children (pre-school)

Young children need to follow a healthy diet so that they grow and stay active. They are growing quickly and need good sources of all nutrients.

Important nutrients needed by young children:

Nutrient	Why it is needed	Sources
Protein	Children grow rapidly at this age	Meat, fish, eggs, milk, cheese, soya
Carbohydrates *(from starchy foods)*	For energy	Bread, pasta, rice, potatoes
Thiamine	To enable children to produce enough energy and to keep up with their level of growth and activity	Red meat, liver, milk, fortified breakfast cereals
Calcium	For healthy bone and teeth development	Milk, cheese, green vegetables
Vitamin D	To work with calcium in bone formation	Sunlight and margarines
Iron	For healthy blood and to keep up with their level of activity	Meat, liver, green vegetables
Vitamin C	To work with iron	Citrus fruits, green vegetables
Fat	For energy and fat-soluble vitamins A, D, E and K	Oily fish, dairy foods

By the time they are about a year old, babies are usually eating the same food as the rest of the family. They should be having three meals a day with healthy snacks in between if they are hungry. This is the best time to develop healthy eating habits that will, hopefully, remain into adulthood. Children like the food they get used to, so it is best to follow the appropriate healthy eating guidelines from a very young age. Children will develop their own likes and dislikes and these should be respected with suitable alternatives being offered. However, children's tastes do change over time, so foods that have been rejected should be tried again another time.

Children need to be taught to develop good eating habits. Many children happily eat a wide range of foods, but most will go through periods of being fussy eaters. Tips to encourage children to eat well include:

1 Set a good example. Children learn by copying what they see, so they need to be shown to eat a wide variety of healthy foods.

2 Eat as a family if possible, with the child having the same food as everyone else so they can develop social skills.

3 Encourage children to feed themselves by providing suitable plates, bowls and cutlery and by making the food easy to eat.

4 Present food attractively so it is appealing to eat.

5 Give small portions and offer more when it is finished. A large plateful can be overwhelming.

6 Get children involved in choosing and preparing meals. They are more likely to eat food if they have been involved.

7 Do not use food as a punishment or reward or bribe; for example, sweets after finishing vegetables, as this gives the message that healthy foods are something to be endured rather than enjoyed.

8 Do not give too many snacks between meals.

9 Do not make a fuss if the child refuses to eat. Healthy children will not starve themselves and refusing to eat may be about seeking attention and testing boundaries, or they may just not be hungry. If the child is active and gaining weight, then they are probably eating enough for their needs.

Activities

1. Suggest three ways in which parents and carers can establish good eating habits in young children.

2. Plan and prepare a meal that you could serve to a young child.

   a) Explain the reasons for your choice.

   b) How would you make the meal attractive to a young child?

   c) Show the nutritional value of the meal.

Check your understanding

1. Name three nutrients young children need and give one example of a food source for each nutrient.

2. Why must babies have iron in their diet when they are weaned?

2.2 School children

When children start attending school they are normally very active and are learning and developing new skills. The general guidelines for healthy eating apply as well as the top tips for feeding younger children.

Research shows that more and more children in Britain are becoming overweight through lack of physical activity linked with a diet with too much sugary and fatty foods.

Balanced meals, a variety of foods and exercise are all important for school children.

Their food should continue to provide them with a good variety and a balance of nutrients. They should have regular meal times and be discouraged from snacking and 'grazing' all day. From the age of about five they can follow the Eatwell plate guidelines and can have semi-skimmed milk or whole milk. Children of this age have 'growth spurts' and may be hungrier than usual when this happens. Their diet should contain plenty of foods that provide protein as well as the minerals needed to make their bones grow. Physical exercise will help the bones take up the minerals and become strong.

Activity

Plan a day's meals for a young child. Give reasons for your choice. Use a nutritional analysis program to compare your menu with the nutritional requirements for a child.

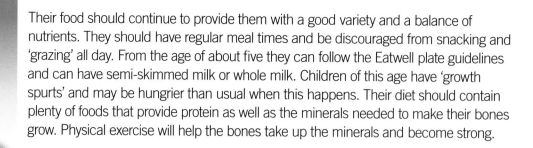

Check your understanding

1. What advice would you give to a parent whose child was refusing to eat?
2. Why is it important that children have plenty of calcium in their diet and exercise?
3. Why do you think there has been an increase in childhood obesity?

2.3 Teenagers

At this stage in life, bodies begin to mature and take on adult form. Growth is usually fast, often occurring in spurts. **Teenagers** need increasing amounts of energy and nutrients for these physical changes. This is something that is described in the Eatwell plate (see Topic 1.1 healthy eating).

A healthy and varied diet is important for growth, and for keeping to a healthy weight. It will also stop people from having serious diseases as they get older. The need for energy is especially important if you are physically active. However, we know from national surveys that adolescents' intake of fatty, sugary and salty foods is well above recommended levels and that **obesity** is a widespread problem among British teenagers. Research also suggests that many teenagers do very little exercise.

The government recommends that young people take part in at least 60 minutes of moderate physical activity every day. It is important to take part in organised sport and exercise. Some sports like cycling, swimming, running should be done twice a week to improve bone health and muscle strength.

Young people grow and develop very quickly and the need for protein is high during this time. Good sources of protein include meat, fish, milk, cheese, eggs, beans, nuts and cereals. This rapid increase in body size and bone growth means that teenagers need more calcium. Without the right amount of calcium they may not have healthy bones as they grow older. Foods rich in calcium and vitamin D should be eaten.

Good sources of calcium include dairy products such as milk, yogurt and cheese. If these foods are not eaten, calcium-fortified soya milk can be a good replacement. In the UK white and brown flour must be **fortified** with calcium. Green vegetables such as broccoli and spring greens also provide calcium. Other good sources are fish that is eaten with the bones such as canned sardines or salmon. Another good source of calcium is calcium enriched mineral water.

Examples of protein foods

In teenage years the need for iron also increases to help with growth and muscle development. Girls need additional supplies to replace the loss of iron through menstruation. Iron from meat sources (known as **haem iron**) (see Topic 1.9 Minerals page 32) such as liver, red meat is readily absorbed by the body. Iron is found in other foods that are not meat. These foods are known as **non-haem iron** foods. Examples of these foods are green leafy vegetables, nuts, wholegrains, pulses and dried fruits. All wheat flours have to be fortified with iron. Many breakfast cereals are also fortified with iron.

A good supply of iron rich foods is important for teenagers

Eating disorders

Eating disorders are typically seen in young girls and increasingly in young boys. They include **anorexia nervosa** and **bulimia nervosa**.

Remember:

- Breakfast is the most important meal of the day.
- Eat three healthy balanced meals a day.
- Daily exercise is important for health.
- Avoid fizzy, carbonated drinks – drink water.
- Do not eat large amounts of processed foods high in sugar, fat and salt.
- Eat natural food – unprocessed, wholegrain cereals, fruit and vegetables, nuts, seeds.

Activities

1. What is the RNI (reference nutrient intake) for girls (11–18) and boys (11–18) for iron and calcium? Say why the amounts for girls and boys are different.

2. What do you think could be done by the government to stop teenagers becoming **overweight** or obese?

Key terms

Teenager – a person aged between 13 and 19.

Obesity – when a person is carrying so much extra weight that it is dangerous for their health.

Fortified – the addition of a nutrient to a food product.

Anorexia nervosa – an eating disorder where people restrict the amount of food they eat.

Bulimia nervosa – an eating disorder where people make themselves vomit after eating to stop themselves putting on weight.

Overweight – when bodyweight is more than that recommended for age and height.

Check your understanding

1. Explain why protein is important for teenagers.

2. Why do teenage girls need good sources of iron in their diet?

3. Explain why calcium is an important mineral for teenagers.

4. Why should teenagers limit the amount of fizzy drinks they consume?

2.4 Older people

As we get older we eat less but it is still necessary to have a well-balanced, varied diet to make sure we get a supply of all the essential vitamins and minerals. Our bodies tend to change with age; we lose muscle and gain fat tissue. This means that we need less energy from foods.

Body **metabolism** slows down as we grow, so we are more likely to gain weight.

It is important for elderly people to be active as it can offer many health benefits. Being physically active can protect against heart disease, stroke, diabetes, some cancers, arthritis and **osteoporosis**. Physical activities can help strengthen muscles and improve bone health. Sometimes general ill-health and having difficulty in chewing means elderly people eat less; they have smaller appetites. They may also have problems with the **digestion** of food.

Older people living alone may need help with planning and preparing meals. Local authorities organise hot midday meals to be delivered to elderly people who have no one else to help them with providing meals.

It is important for elderly people not to have too much salt in their diet. No more than 6g a day is the amount recommended. It is the sodium part of salt that is bad for health and having too much sodium in our diet can cause fluid to be kept in the body. This can raise blood pressure, and raised blood pressure is dangerous because it can cause strokes and heart disease. Cutting down salt in the diet can be very easy. Cut out or cut down on salty foods such as bacon, cheese, pickles, smoked fish, bottled sauces, vegetables and fish canned in brine. Use reduced salt products where possible and use herbs and spices such as garlic, ginger, lemon or lime to flavour meals instead of adding salt.

Elderly people need to eat foods rich in calcium for strong bones. This is especially important for older women as their bone strength tends to be weaker than men, particularly if they've given birth. Good sources of calcium rich foods are dairy products, fish where the bones can be eaten, soya products and fortified breakfast cereals.

It is more difficult for the body to absorb some nutrients in old age. A good example of this is vitamin B12. A diet containing plenty of B vitamins, particularly B6, B12 and folic acid is very important for health and may help prevent heart disease or dementia in old age.

Good food sources of these B vitamins are:

Folic acid (folate) – fruit and vegetable, wholegrains, beans, breakfast cereals.

B6 – fortified cereals, beans, poultry, fish.

B12 – fish, poultry, meat, eggs, dairy produce, fortified breakfast cereals, soya milk.

Key terms

Metabolism – a set of reactions needed to keep the body working.

Osteoporosis – a disease where the bones become weak and can break easily.

Digestion – the process of food travelling through the body and being used by the body for various functions.

Examples of good food sources of B vitamins

Top tips for older people:

1 Eat an enjoyable and varied diet.

2 Eat plenty of fruit and vegetables.

3 Include oily fish in the diet.

4 Get enough fibre.

5 Reduce salt intake.

6 Eat calcium rich foods.

7 Boost B vitamins.

8 Stay active and keep your brain active.

9 Drink plenty of water.

Check your understanding

1. Why do people tend to need less energy-giving foods as they get older?
2. Why is it important for elderly people to eat foods rich in calcium?
3. How can elderly people cut down on the amount of salt in their diet?

2.5 Pregnant women

It is important for a woman who is pregnant to follow the same normal healthy eating guidelines that are given to everyone. This means she should eat foods from the four main food groups every day – you may have heard of the phrase 'eating for two', but there is no need for women to do this. Her body will simply adapt to use whatever nutrients it gets for both her and her baby. A good intake of folic acid is important too (see page 28 on folate).

Foods to choose

Nutrient	Why it is needed	Sources
Starchy, fibre rich food	Energy needs increase a little in the last three months of pregnancy, and she should have about 200kcal extra per day	Wholemeal bread and cereals
Vitamin D	You absorb the calcium and prevent low birth weight	Sunlight, oily fish and margarine
Folic acid (folate)	Reducing the risk of the baby developing defects in the spine, known as spina bifida	Breakfast cereals and bread, green vegetables
Calcium	Helps with growth of the skeleton and bones	Dairy foods, white bread, green vegetables
Iron	Helps with the baby's growth and prevents anaemia in mother	Red meat, green vegetables
Dietary fibre	Prevents constipation and piles	Wholegrain foods and vegetables
Protein	For baby's growth	Meat, fish, eggs, milk, soya
Vitamin C	Helps with absorption of iron	Citrus fruits

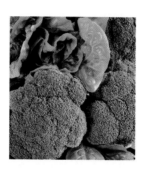 

Foods containing folic acid

Foods to avoid

There are some foods that women should avoid when they are pregnant, mainly because they could harm the baby. These foods may contain food poisoning bacteria such as **Salmonella** and **Listeria**. If a pregnant woman eats food containing these bacteria, it can cause serious illness and may lead to miscarriage or early delivery of the baby.

Foods which may contain *Salmonella* are:

- Uncooked meats
- Uncooked vegetables
- Unpasteurised milk and yogurt and cheese made from unpasteurised milk
- Some chilled ready meals.

Foods which may contain *Listeria* are:

- Raw and lightly cooked meat and poultry
- Paté
- Raw eggs and any food containing raw eggs such as homemade mayonnaise, and some desserts
- Soft and blue-veined cheeses (e.g. Brie, Stilton).

Liver and liver products (e.g. paté) and any supplements that have fish oils all contain high amounts of vitamin A. Vitamin A is stored in the body and a build-up is toxic to the baby, causing birth defects.

Some types of fish, such as swordfish, marlin and shark, contain high levels of mercury, which can harm the baby's nervous system and should be avoided. Tuna also contains mercury, so a pregnant woman should limit her intake to no more than two tuna steaks or four medium cans of tuna a week.

Good food hygiene is essential to prevent food poisoning. Food poisoning can have long-term consequences for the unborn baby, even if the mother is not very ill.

Activity

Plan, prepare and cook a healthy meal containing folic acid that would be suitable for an expectant mother.

Check your understanding

1. Describe how a pregnant woman can make sure she has a healthy diet.
2. Identify the foods an expectant mother should avoid. Give reasons for your answer.

Key terms

Salmonella and *Listeria* – food poisoning bacteria.

2.6 Weight loss diets

The number of people who are overweight and obese is increasing in the UK. Obesity is caused when a person takes in more energy from food. This extra energy is then stored as body fat. Sugary and fatty foods are high energy foods: the energy from food is measured in calories. A diet aimed at losing weight means eating less high calorie food and drink.

Energy balance is when we take in the same amount of energy from food as the energy we use up during the day. If we take in more energy from food than we need, we become overweight. If we take in less energy from food than we need, we lose weight.

There are several reasons why people need to lose weight. The most common reasons are linked to health conditions such as CHD (coronary heart disease), type 2 diabetes, high blood pressure, stroke, arthritis, more strain on joints and breathing problems. Obesity can also cause people to have low self-esteem.

The method used to work out if you are overweight is called **BMI** (body mass index). You can tell from your BMI whether you are underweight, a healthy weight, overweight or obese.

If you need to lose weight, you need to take in fewer energy-giving foods or fewer calories than the energy or calories used by the body. There are several ways to do this. Change4life gives ideas on how to lose weight and eat healthily. Losing weight should be a gradual process and it often takes a long time before results can be seen.

Counting calories is one method of losing weight

Key term

BMI – a method for estimating body fat.

47

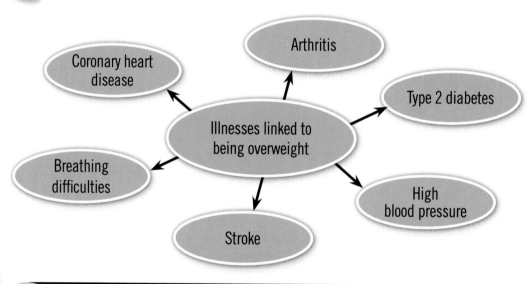

Weight maintenance

Weight gain

Weight loss

Food intake

Energy expenditure

'Obesity is the greatest public health crisis affecting the UK.'
'One in five of primary school children in the UK is obese.'

Remember:

- Reduce sugary and fatty foods.
- Eat more low energy foods, wholegrain cereals.
- Change methods of cooking to grilling, steaming, microwaving and baking instead of frying.
- Use lower in fat options: cheese, bacon, spreads, milk.
- Use sugar free and lower in sugar options – drinks.
- Increase exercise, be more active.

Coronary heart disease

Arthritis

Type 2 diabetes

Illnesses linked to being overweight

Breathing difficulties

Stroke

High blood pressure

Activities

1. Find out how body mass index is worked out.

2. Explain the difference between being overweight and obesity.

Check your understanding

1. What is meant by the term obese?

2. Explain how a person can become overweight.

3. What does a person need to do to lose weight?

4. Complete the following sentences:

 a) Losing weight means cutting down on ...... and ..... foods.

 b) .... is a healthier method of cooking than frying.

 c) Drink ..... instead of fizzy drinks.

 d) The size and weight of food we eat is called a ....

2.7 Vegetarians

Vegetarians are people who choose not to eat meat, poultry, game or any animal product such as offal (liver, heart, kidney) and gelatine or fish where an animal, bird or fish has been killed.

There are a variety of reasons why people choose to follow a vegetarian diet:

- Eating flesh of a living creature is not acceptable to them.
- They do not agree with the killing of animals, birds and fish – they may object to the cruelty of slaughtering animals or animal welfare.
- Environmental issues – they think using land, energy and food to rear animals is wasteful.
- They consider a vegetarian diet to be healthier option.
- Many vegetarians do not eat meat, fish or animal products for religious reasons.
- Peer pressure or media pressure.

Types of vegetarians:

Lacto-ovo vegetarians do not eat flesh (meat, poultry and fish) but will eat eggs and dairy foods such as milk, butter, cheese, cream and yogurt.

Lacto-vegetarians do not eat flesh or eggs but will eat dairy foods.

Vegans do not eat any animal foods, food products or bee products such as honey. They are often called strict vegetarians because they will only eat plant foods such as cereals, nuts, seeds, pulses (peas, beans, lentils) as well as fruit and vegetables.

Vegetarian diets are often bulky because they rely on cereals, pulses, nuts and seeds for their protein. These foods are high in dietary fibre (see page 35 on dietary fibre). Vegetarian diets can be very healthy as they are usually low in fat and high in dietary fibre. Vegetarian diets can also be unhealthy because some vegetarians eat a lot of high fat dairy products.

It is important that all vegetarians take omega 3 supplements as their diet does not include oily fish, which is the only source in the diet.

As is the case with everyone, vegetarians should eat a variety of foods and have a balanced diet (see Topic 1.1 on healthy eating). There are some nutrients that need special mention. These are protein, iron (vegans especially), zinc, selenium and some of the B vitamins.

Protein should not be a problem if a wide variety of foods are eaten. All the essential amino acids are found in animal foods, and plant proteins have a low content of one or more of the essential amino acids needed by the body. Soya and quinoa are the only vegetarian sources which contain good amounts of all the essential amino acids. Good sources of plan protein include pulses (lentils, beans) nuts and seeds, cereals and mycoprotein (sold as Quorn).

Key terms

Lacto-ovo vegetarian – vegetarians who do not eat meat, but eat eggs and dairy produce

Lacto-vegetarian – vegetarians who do not eat meat, fish or eggs but eat dairy products.

Vegan – vegetarians who do not eat any food from animals.

Hummus paté with pitta bread

Stuffed peppers with couscous

A mixed bean salad

Lentil soup

There are other types of meat alternatives available which are suitable for vegetarians and vegans.

A diet based on a mixture of plant foods can still provide an individual with a good supply of protein.

Iron can be deficient in a vegan diet as the best source of iron is meat. Good sources of iron include pulses, green vegetables such as watercress, broccoli and leafy green vegetables, bread and fortified breakfast cereal. This type of iron (non-haem) is less easily absorbed by the body. Eating a vitamin C rich food at the same time as an iron rich food helps with the absorption of iron. Many vegetarians buy iron supplements to ensure they do not become deficient in iron and develop anaemia. It is also important for vegetarians to include plenty of fresh fruit and vegetables in the diet to help the body absorb the iron.

Good foods rich in zinc and selenium are important for the immune system. Zinc is found in dairy products, pulses, wholegrain cereals; selenium is found in nuts.

Vitamin B12 is needed to make red blood cells and keeps the nervous system healthy. Dairy products and eggs are good sources, also yeast extract, soya milk, sunflower margarine and breakfast cereals all of which are fortified with this nutrient.

Food labelling claims include 'meat free', 'suitable for vegetarians/vegans' and 'free from dairy foods/eggs'.

Vegetarian food products cannot by law be made in the same place as products containing meat.

www.vegsoc.org

Activities

1. Name two nutrients that may be lacking in a vegetarian diet and identify a range of foods that might supply these nutrients.

2. A group of students are making lunches for a group of elderly people who live alone and who find it difficult to cook for themselves. Plan tasty, healthy two-course lunch menus for these elderly people for five days.

Check your understanding

1. What term is used to describe a person who will not eat meat, fish or any product that comes from or is made from these foods?

2. What is the term used to describe a person who will not eat meat, fish eggs or product that comes from or is made from these foods.

3. What is the term used to describe a person who will not eat dairy products, eggs or anything that comes from an animal.

Stretch and challenge

1. Breakfast is the most important meal of the day for teenagers yet many teenagers do not eat breakfast.

   a) Why do you think teenagers skip breakfast?

   b) Explain why eating breakfast is considered to be a good start to the day.

2. a) Find out what peak bone mass is.

   b) Why do you think old people are more likely than younger people to suffer from bone fractures?

3. Doctors have called for a new tax on soft drinks and the banning of advertising of foods high in saturated fat, sugar and salt before 9 p.m. in order to tackle the growing problem of obesity (*The Independent* 04/03/13).

   a) Give reasons why doctors have suggested the above measures on tax and the ban on advertising.

   b) Do you think these measures would help in tackling the problem of obesity? Give reasons for your answer.

4. Read the following article on obesity:

'Britain has more overweight people than anywhere else in Europe, according to a recent survey. Being overweight or obese is linked to the risk of developing life-threatening illnesses such as heart disease, diabetes, high blood pressure and osteoarthritis. There is also evidence to show that overweight people are more likely to develop certain types of cancer.

The cost of treating obesity-related illnesses to the NHS is estimated to be around £2.6 billion a year.

Other studies have shown that the percentage of overweight children in Britain has virtually doubled in the last decade.

The growing problem of obesity-related illnesses points towards an unhealthy diet and lifestyle.'

   a) Identify the health risks that are linked to overweight and obesity.

   b) What are the reasons for people becoming overweight and obese?

   c) Describe other factors that are blamed for overweight and obesity.

   d) Explain why obesity can cost so much money to the NHS.

2.8 Food allergies and intolerances

Many people have an unpleasant reaction to specific foods. A food allergy and a food intolerance both cause unpleasant reactions or symptoms in the body.

An allergy is a type of intolerance which involves the body's immune system. It is often a serious reaction to a specific ingredient in foods such as strawberries, nuts and gluten. It occurs when the body does not produce enough of the particular chemical needed for the digestion of that food.

Key term

Anaphylactic shock – a very serious condition when the body develops a swelling in the throat and mouth.

Wheat, barley and rye contain gluten

An allergic reaction is caused when the food is eaten or touched. It could take minutes or hours for the reaction to take place and it can be very serious. A severe reaction may result in **anaphylactic shock.**

The following foods are examples of those known to cause allergies:

- Peanuts
- Eggs
- Strawberries.

The symptoms of an allergy are skin rash, itchy skin, runny nose, swollen lips and face, wheezing and coughing.

A food Intolerance is when the body is not able to completely break down food to be absorbed. It often happens because the body lacks a particular enzyme for this process to take place. The unabsorbed food then remains in the digestive system causing symptoms of bloating, cramps, feeling sick and diarrhoea.

An example of food intolerance is lactose intolerance.

Food allergies and intolerances are common in children, especially those under the age of three. They can vary considerable in severity and the length of time they last. Peanut allergy, for example, usually lasts a lifetime and can cause serious life-threatening reactions to tiny amounts of peanut protein. Lactose (cows' milk) intolerance may be severe in early life but typically disappears as the child grows older.

Lactose intolerance

Lactose intolerance can cause bloating of the abdomen and diarrhoea. People who are lactose intolerant lack or have low levels of the enzyme lactase which is needed to digest the sugar lactose found in milk ready to be absorbed into the large intestine. It is a condition commonly seen in young children. People with this condition must avoid milk and milk products and use other types of milk or soya milk.

Coeliac disease

Coeliac disease is usually a life-long condition requiring a life-long and strict **gluten-free** diet. The main organ affected is the small intestine, when the gluten causes inflammation and damage. People who suffer from coeliac disease are unable to eat foods containing wheat, barley, oats and rye because their bodies cannot tolerate the protein **gluten** found in these cereals. If they eat these foods, the gluten damages the lining of the small intestine, preventing the absorption of nutrients and they lose weight.

Coeliac disease is also called gluten intolerance and it has a wide range of symptoms. It is a condition which cannot be cured but it can be controlled by a suitable gluten-free diet.

All foods containing wheat, barley, oats and rye must be removed from the diet of a person suffering from coeliac disease. Wheat flour, in particular, has a high gluten content and this means that people with coeliac disease cannot eat foods such as bread, many breakfast cereals, pasta and pizza. Many processed foods also contain gluten products and, by law, packaged food products have to carry a full list of the ingredients they contain.

Many ingredients are known to cause allergic reactions. All pre-packed foods sold in the UK have to show clearly on the label if they contain one of the following: peanuts, nuts, eggs, milk, crustaceans (prawns, crab and lobster), mollusc (squid, mussels, cockles, whelks, snails), fish, sesame seeds, cereals containing gluten, soya, celery, mustard, sulphur dioxide.

This information can help the consumer identify whether or not a food contains an ingredient that they need to avoid. Many food products also carry an allergy warning on the label.

Gluten free information

Labelling symbol for gluten-free products

Many products are available specially produced for coeliac sufferers and there are alternative ingredients available for food preparation. Some are listed below.

Name of food	What it is used for
Agar	Instead of gelatine to set desserts
Almonds	Used in cakes and biscuits instead of flour
Buckwheat	To make flour and noodles
Carrageenan	Used as a thickener and stabiliser in foods
Cassava	Used as a cereal and as a thickener
Chestnuts	Ground up and used as flour
Corn (maize)	Used as a flour and thickener
Gram flour	Made from chick peas and used in a variety of dishes instead of using wheat flour
Linseeds	Can be added to foods such as breakfast cereals to improve the nutritional content
Millet	Often used as a muesli and added to other foods
Mustard	Used as a seed, an oil and flour in a variety of dishes
Peas, beans, lentils	Made into flours and used for a variety of dishes
Polenta	Made from boiled corn meal and used in cakes, puddings and savoury dishes
Potato flour	Can be used in cakes, pastries and biscuits and as a thickener
Quinoa	Used in baking and as an alternative to rice or couscous
Rice	Used either whole, flaked or ground in many dishes
Sago	Used as a thickener or pudding
Sorghum	Used as a cereal or a source of syrup
Soya	Used in biscuits, cakes and pastries

2.9 Diabetes

Diabetes is one of the major causes of premature illness and death. There are two main types: type 1 and type 2.

Type 1 – where the immune system of the body turns against itself causing damage to the cells that make insulin. It is often called juvenile diabetes or early-onset diabetes because it often develops before the age of 40, usually during the teenage years.

Type 2 – develops either because the body does not produce enough insulin or the insulin does not work properly. This type is on the increase especially amongst younger people. Diabetes is thought to be linked to more people being overweight as a result of eating too many sugary and fatty foods, not enough fibre and not exercising enough.

Diabetes occurs when the amount of glucose (blood sugar) is too high. Blood sugar is controlled in the body by the hormone called insulin. Diabetes means that the person's body is either not producing any insulin or that the body is not able to use the insulin to control the glucose level.

There is no cure for diabetes but it can be managed by diet and medication. To prevent the development of diabetes it is recommended that people eat a balanced diet following the Eatwell plate guidelines, increase physical activity and exercise and maintain a healthy weight.

It is important that diabetics read food labels to determine whether products contain hidden sugars, which are often listed under their chemical names: sucrose, dextrose, fructose, maltodextrin, glucose syrup.

2.10 Coronary heart disease

Cardiovascular disease (CVD) or coronary heart disease (CHD), which includes heart disease and stroke, remains one of the main causes of death and ill-health in the UK. It is caused when the coronary arteries which supply blood to the heart become narrower.

Atherosclerosis is a process that causes narrowing of the blood vessels. It happens when a type of fat in the blood called low density lipoprotein cholesterol (LDL cholesterol) gathers in the blood vessel wall causing 'furring'. The wall becomes thicker and prevents the correct flow of blood through the vessels to the heart. This may cause chest pain which is known as angina.

Thrombosis occurs when a large clot forms in the blood vessels, stopping blood from reaching the heart. It leads to a heart attack and if the blood cannot get to the brain this leads to a stroke.

Important risk factors for heart disease include obesity, high blood pressure, high blood cholesterol and type 2 diabetes.

To reduce the risk of CHD it is important to eat a varied diet following healthy eating guidelines (Eatwell plate) including five or more portions of fruit and vegetables a day, reducing intake of saturated fat, salt and eating two portions of fish, one of which should be oily fish, every week.

2.11 Bowel disorders

These include:

Constipation – caused by lack of dietary fibre and water in the diet.

Diverticular disease – a problem linked to constipation. A high fibre diet with plenty of fruit and vegetables will help in treating the disorder.

Bowel cancers – linked to obesity, diet, smoking, alcohol, digestive disorders, lack of exercise and family history. Research suggests that a diet high in fat and red meat and low in fibre, fruit and vegetables can increase the risk of bowel cancers.

2.12 Bone and joint health

Bone mass increases with age until our early twenties when it is at its maximum. From the age of about forty bone mass decreases. Excessive loss of bone mass leads to osteoporosis developing in later life characterised by weak, fragile bones.

A number of nutrients are important for strong healthy bones, in particular, calcium, vitamin D and vitamin K. An active lifestyle is also important.

Check your understanding

1. Name a health condition caused by a diet:
   a) High in sugary foods.
   b) Low in calcium and vitamin D.
   c) Lacking in dietary fibre.
2. What is coronary heart disease (CHD)?
3. Describe the changes that a person could make to their diet to lower the risk of developing CHD.

Stretch and challenge

1. Explain why a person with diabetes should eat more wholemeal and wholegrain foods such as bread, rice and breakfast cereals.

2. Plan a two-course evening meal that is suitable for a coeliac. Give reasons for your choice.

Activities

1. Study the following information found on food labels. Describe the meaning of each:
   - Gluten free.
   - Sugar free.
   - Lactose free.
   - Vegan.

2. Prepare a poster for your local health clinic giving advice to people on how to prevent CHD.

Exam practice

1. Joe is a 15-year-old who takes a packed lunch to school. These are the foods he usually puts into his lunch box:

   A sausage roll

   A packet of salted crisps

   A cheese and mayonnaise sandwich (white bread)

   A chocolate digestive biscuit

   An apple

   A can of coke.

   a) Do you think Joe's choice of food and drink is a healthy choice? Give reasons for your answer. [6]

   b) What improvements would you make to his packed lunch? Give reasons why you would make these changes. [4]

2. Many people are choosing not to include meat in the diet.

   a) Explain the reasons for not including meat in the diet. [6]

   b) Give advice to a teenager, who has decided not to include meat in his diet, on how to maintain a balanced diet. [6]

3. About 5% of the UK population consider themselves to be vegetarians, according to a recent survey.

   a) Give reasons why a person decides to become a vegetarian. [4]

   b) Suggest how to make the following dishes suitable for a lacto-vegetarian. [4]

   (i) A beef lasagne.

   (ii) A lemon cheesecake (set with gelatine).

4. Diet can be a contributing factor to deficiency disease.

   Discuss the importance of calcium in the diet. [6]

5. Why is it important for consumers to read the ingredients list on a food label? [6]

Topic 3: Food commodities

What will I learn?

- The structure and how individual foods are made up.
- The variety and types of food available.
- Nutritional value.
- Using the food in practical work.
- Choosing the food and using it safely.

Understanding about food commodities will help you to use food successfully in practical tasks.

3.1 Meat and poultry

Meat comes from animals. Poultry is the name of the meat that comes from birds. Examples of meat are beef, lamb, veal, pork, bacon and ham. Examples of poultry are chicken, turkey and duck.

Examples of products which are made from meat and poultry are sausages, burgers, rissoles, salami.

Offal is the name given to the internal organs of animals. Examples are liver, kidney, heart.

Duck, goose, chicken

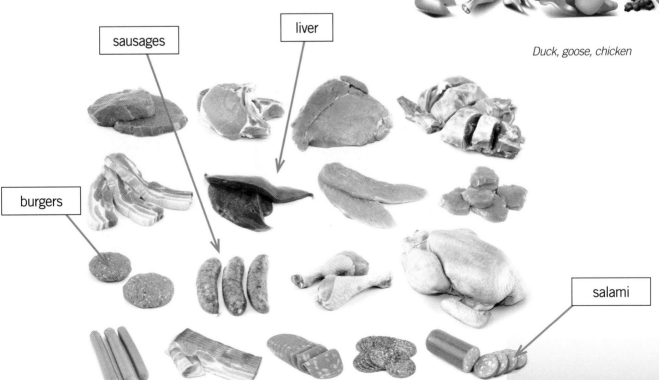

A selection of meats, meat products and offal

A pork chop   *A lamb chop*

A lean beef steak (showing no fat)

Beef steak showing marbling (fat spread throughout the lean meat)

Nutritional value

Meat and poultry meat are made up of muscle and nutrients. The amount of nutrients varies according to the age of the animal or bird, the part of the animal or bird which is eaten and the way the animal or bird has been kept and fed.

Meat and poultry is made up of water, protein and fat, Vitamin A and D, B group of vitamins, iron and water.

The protein in meat and poultry is an important source of **high biological value** (HBV) protein. Offal is an excellent source of HBV protein.

> ### Key term
>
> **High biological value** – protein food which has all the essential amino acids.

Heart

Liver

Kidney

The amount of fat in meat and poultry varies. We can see the fat on the meat; it lies beneath the skin and is found in-between muscle fibre. Meat tends to have more fat than poultry. Most of the fat is saturated fat.

To lower the fat:

- Do not add extra fat when cooking.
- Dry fry mince and pour away the fat.
- Remove skin on chicken.
- Choose lean varieties.
- Cut off visible fat.

There is some vitamin A and D in meat. The more fat in the meat, the more vitamin A and D there is. Liver, kidney, heart are very good sources of vitamin A and D.

Pregnant women are advised not to eat liver during the early stages of pregnancy as it may cause harm to the foetus.

Meat and poultry are good sources of B vitamins; heart and kidney are excellent sources of vitamin B1. Red meat is an important source of iron. Liver is a particularly good source of iron. Chicken also contains vitamins B6 and B12 and the mineral selenium.

Buying meat and poultry

Buy from a reliable source. Meat and poultry should be a good colour, firm and slightly springy to touch. Always check the use by date on pre-packed meat and poultry.

Poultry produced in the UK is reared in different ways, for example:

- Indoors in large numbers and not allowed out; a standard chicken is about 40 days old when it is slaughtered.
- Free-range – where the chickens are kept in large sheds but are allowed outside; these are about 56 days old when they are slaughtered.
- Organic – where chickens are allowed to roam and are fed on organic food; these are about 80 days old when slaughtered. They are also more expensive to buy.

Free range or barn hens

There are symbols on packaging to show that meat and poultry have met welfare standards:

The RSPCA welfare label

Animal welfare labels

Battery hens

Storing meat and poultry

Meat and poultry are perishable foods. Poultry is a high risk food because it contains bacteria and therefore correct storage is important.

If bought in plastic packaging, the wrapping should be removed and the meat or poultry placed on a plate, covered or in a container with a lid in the refrigerator held at below 5°C. Raw meat should be stored at the bottom of the refrigerator.

Poultry carries bacteria such as *Salmonella* which can easily pass from one food to another. Care should be taken that the poultry does not touch other foods in the refrigerator.

Activity

Compare the nutritional value of protein per 100g for beef, pork, lamb and chicken.

Comment on your findings.

Check your understanding

1. What is the nutritional value of meat and poultry?
2. Give advice on storing fresh meat and poultry.
3. Name four meat products.

3.2 Fish and seafood

Fish and seafood are either caught from the sea or freshwater rivers and lakes or they are reared in large numbers on fish farms.

There are three types of fish and seafood:

- White fish
- Oily fish
- Shellfish
  - Molluscs
  - Crustaceans.

Shellfish

White fish has:

- firm white flesh
- oil in the liver, not in the flesh.

Examples are cod, coley, hake, haddock, halibut, monkfish, plaice, sea bass, sole, tilapia, and whiting.

Oily fish has:

- oil in the flesh
- a dark colour.

Examples are anchovy, herring, mackerel, pilchard, salmon, sardine, trout, tuna, whitebait.

Shellfish:

- Molluscs are little sea creatures that live inside shells. Examples are clams, cockles, mussels, oysters, scallops.
- Crustaceans are sea creatures with joints and soft bodies covered by hard shells. Examples are crabs, crayfish, langoustines, lobster, prawns, and shrimps.

Different types of white and oily fish

Nutritional value

Fish and seafood have the following nutrients:

Protein, fat, vitamin A and D, B vitamins, calcium, fluoride, iodine, water.

Fish and seafood are an excellent source of high biological value protein which can be easily digested. (See Topic 1.5 on Proteins on page 18.)

The fat in fish is in the form of unsaturated oils. Oily fish provides the essential **omega 3 fatty acids** which are known to reduce the risk of heart disease and reduce cholesterol levels. Whitefish have less than 5% fat; oily fish have 10–20% fat in their flesh. (See Topic 1.7 Fats and oils on pages 23–25.)

- Oily fish are good sources of vitamin A and D. The liver oils of white fish also contain vitamin A and D and the oil is processed and sold as cod liver oil capsules and halibut liver oil capsules.
- Fish and shellfish both contain B vitamins.
- Tinned fish can contain edible bones and these are a good source of calcium.
- Sea fish provide useful amounts of fluoride and iodine.

We should eat at least two portions of fish a week to give us a range of minerals and vitamins, as well as protein. One of these portions should be an oily fish such as fresh or tinned salmon, mackerel or sardines because they contain omega 3 fatty acids. Fresh or frozen tuna is also rich in omega 3.

Omega 3 fish oil capsules

Canned fish is rich in omega 3

Buying fish and shellfish

- Fresh – fishmonger or supermarket.
- Frozen – fish is cut into portions and frozen soon after it is caught.
- Canned – tinned in brine, oil or a sauce, e.g. salmon, mackerel, sardines, tuna.
- Smoked – preserved fish with a different taste, e.g. trout, salmon.
- Dried – preserved fish, e.g. cod.
- Pickled – preserved in vinegar, e.g. rollmop herring.

Buy fish from a reliable source. Make sure that fresh fish has firm flesh, moist skin and has a fresh clean smell.

Fish and seafood are perishable, high risk foods and 'go off' very quickly. If bought fresh, they need to be refrigerated and used as soon as possible.

Fish cooks very quickly. During cooking the muscles in the fish shrink and moisture escapes. The **connective tissue** is called collagen and this changes to gelatine during cooking.

Cutlets of fresh fish

Sustainability of fish

Many of our fish stocks are reducing because:

- Too many fish are being taken out of our seas and oceans.
- Too much rubbish is being thrown in the sea and too little is being done to protect marine wildlife.

Many people prefer to eat fish that comes from a sustainable source, that is, from managed stocks and is caught and farmed in a way that causes minimal damage to the environment and other wildlife.

Fillets of fresh fish

Key terms

Omega 3 fatty acids – important for a healthy heart.

Connective tissue – tissue which holds together, connects and surrounds body parts.

Activities

1. Explain why it is recommended that we eat two portions of fish a week, one of which should be an oily fish.

2. Find out more about the sustainability of fish – where your seafood comes from, the issues facing our seas and oceans and why making the right choices is good for us.

Stretch and challenge

Write an article for a supermarket magazine promoting the value of fish in the diet.

Check your understanding

1. Name two examples of white fish.
2. Name two examples of oily fish.
3. Name two examples of shellfish.
4. What is the nutritional value of fish?

3.3 Milk

Cows' milk is the most widely used in the UK, although goat and sheep milk is available.

Milk is produced on farms and sent to be processed, to be put into bottles or cartons and sold as liquid milk. Milk is also sold in tins, as powder, and made into cheese, yogurt, butter and cream.

Nutritional value of milk

Babies are fed milk usually for the first few months until weaned on to solid food. It must therefore have everything that the baby needs to grow, give energy and help protect against infection and disease.

Milk contains high biological value protein. It is an excellent source of calcium with good amounts of phosphorus, sodium and potassium. It does not, however, contain iron but babies are born with a store of iron from the mother until weaned.

The amount of fat in milk depends on type. Cows' whole milk naturally contains about 3% fat. Milk contains a little carbohydrate in the form of sugar known as lactose, which gives it a slightly sweet taste.

- Milk is 90% water and contains water-soluble B vitamins.
- Vitamin A and D are found in milk, the amount depending on the fat content.
- There is no fibre or vitamin C in milk.

Milk and milk products

Types of milk

Whole, untreated milk has a cream line on top. Before being sold, the milk goes through a process called **homogenisation**. This process breaks up the fat layer so that it mixes with the rest of the milk and does not float on top.

The fat content of milk varies according to type:

- Whole milk has about 4% fat.
- Semi-skimmed milk has about 1.7% fat, about half the fat of whole milk.
- Skimmed milk has 0.1–0.3% fat, which is almost fat free.

Milk will spoil easily because it is easily and quickly affected by bacteria, which can make it 'go off'. For this reason milk is treated with heat to destroy harmful bacteria. There are many ways to heat treat milk:

- **Pasteurisation** where the milk is heated to 72°C for 15 seconds and then cooled quickly and then bottled or put into cartons. The milk must be refrigerated and used within a few days once opened.
- **Ultra-heat treat** or UHT where the milk is heated to a very high temperature (132°C) for a second and then quickly cooled and packed. This is also known as long-life milk and is available in sealed packs. The milk keeps for several months if unopened, but once opened must be used within a few days.
- **Dried or powdered** milk where the milk is mixed with water before using.

Key terms

Homogenisation – a process which breaks down the fat globules in milk.

Pasteurisation – a heating process to kill harmful bacteria in milk.

Ultra heat treated – a process carried out to extend shelf life of a food.

● **Canned milk** where the milk is heated to evaporate some of the water, sealed in cans and heated to sterilise it. Evaporated milk, sold in cans is not sweetened. Condensed milk, sold in cans, has sugar added to it and is very thick.

There are a growing number of other milks on the market which have been produced from plants to cater for vegans and people with allergies. These include soya, oat, rice and coconut milk, which are fortified with vitamin and minerals.

Activities

1. Many children do not want or like to drink milk. Suggest ways of including milk in the diet of children.

2. Semi-skimmed milk is the most popular type of milk in the UK. Discuss the reasons for this trend.

Check your understanding

1. Explain why milk is such an important food.

2. What is the difference between whole milk, semi-skimmed milk and skimmed milk?

3.4 Dairy products

Milk can be made into a variety of products such as cheese, yogurt, cream and butter.

Cheese

Cheese can be made from cow, goat, ewe or buffalo milk. Whole or semi-skimmed milk can be used to make cheese. There is a variety of cheese available from different countries.

A selection of cheeses

Nutritional value of cheese

The main nutrients in cheese are protein, fat, vitamins, minerals and water. The amounts of these nutrients vary according to the type of milk used to make the cheese and the way the cheese is made.

Cheese is a good source of protein and calcium as well as the minerals phosphorus, zinc and magnesium. Cheese provides the B group of vitamins and some vitamin A and D. The amount of fat in cheese varies according to type: hard cheese is about 33% fat, cream cheese is about 50% fat, whilst cottage cheese is about 4% fat. It is possible to buy low fat or fat reduced cheeses. There is no carbohydrate, fibre or vitamin C in cheese.

All types of cheese should be stored in the refrigerator in a sealed container or packaging to prevent it from drying out.

Examples of cheese dishes

Lasagne

Greek pasta dish using feta cheese

Quiche

Macaroni cheese

A cheesecake using soft cream cheese or cottage cheese

Cheese has many uses in cooking. The fat in the cheese separates from the protein at about 65°C and the cheese melts and spreads. It melts more easily when grated and can be mixed with a starchy food such as breadcrumbs to absorb the fat.

If the heat is too high, it overcooks and the cheese becomes hard and tough. When this happens, it smells acrid (bitter).

Examples of types of cheeses:

Type of cheese	Examples
Hard	Cheddar, Cheshire, Derby, Double Gloucester, Gruyere, Gouda, Emmental, Parmesan (very hard)
Semi-soft	Gorgonzola, Wensleydale, Lancashire, Caerphilly, Edam, St Paulin, Bel Paese
Blue-vein (blue coloured veins or mould through the cheese)	Stilton, Danish Blue, Cambozola
Fresh	Cream cheese, cottage cheese, quark, curd cheese, Boursin, Le Roule, fromage frais, mascarpone, mozzarella, feta, halloumi
Ripened	Camembert, Brie, goat's cheese
Whey	Ricotta
Processed	Cheese slices, cheese spreads, cheese strings

Mozzarella cheese on a pizza topping

Yogurt

Yogurt is made from warm milk which has had a bacteria culture added to it. The bacteria acts on the lactose (sugar) turning it into lactic acid. This gives yogurt its tangy, slightly sour taste. The lactic acid sets the protein and the yogurt thickens.

There are many varieties of yogurt depending on the type of milk used and the extra ingredients added during the making. Plain yogurt is natural. Fruit, sugar and other ingredients such as honey may be added. Yogurt drinks are also available and natural yogurt is the main ingredient in the Indian drink 'lassi'.

Nutritional value of yogurt

Yogurt is a useful source of high biological value protein. The amount of fat in yogurt varies according to type. Yogurts are available as low fat, very low fat and fat free because they are made from skimmed milk. Some yogurts have cream added making them fairly high in fat content. All yogurts contain calcium, B vitamins as well as some vitamin A and D.

Types of yogurt

Set – semi-solid and set in the pot. Can be natural or fruit flavoured.

Stirred yogurt – can be poured from the pot. Can be natural or flavoured.

Natural or plain – smooth and creamy, with a tangy flavour.

Greek yogurt – made from cows' or ewes' milk. Has a mild flavour and a high fat content.

Live yogurt – the bacteria is still living. These are good to aid digestion.

Dairy products

Cream

Cream is the fat in milk. The fat is skimmed off the milk at a temperature of 35ºC to 54ºC and cooled very quickly to 4ºC.

There are many varieties of cream and they vary according to the amount of fat they contain. Lower in fat options are available.

Nutritional value of cream

Cream contains fat, the amount varying according to type (see chart). It contains a small amount of protein, some vitamin A and D and calcium.

Name of cream (fat content)	Use and description
Single cream 18% fat	Pouring on desserts In coffee Added to soups and sauces
Whipping cream 38% fat	Good for whisking Used to decorate desserts and cakes
Double cream 48% fat	Whisking and decorating Pouring over desserts Making ice cream
Soured cream 20% fat slightly tangy	Dips Sauces Adding to soups Topping such as jacket potatoes
Crème fraiche 35% fat	Desserts Dips Cheesecakes Adding to mashed potato Cannot be whipped
Clotted cream 55% fat from Jersey or Guernsey cows	Traditionally served with jam on scones With desserts
Ready whipped cream	Sold in aerosols and heat treated to last longer Used to decorate desserts

Butter

Butter is made from the cream of the milk. It is used for spreading and cooking and has a good flavour.

Nutritional value of butter

Butter is mostly fat, which is saturated. There is vitamin A and D in butter, more when the milk comes from cows which have grazed on grass in the summer months.

Types of butter:

Name of butter	Description
Unsalted	Mild and slightly sweet and sold in a wrapped block
Salted	Salt added for flavour, sold in a wrapped block
Clarified	Butter is melted and the clear fat on top is used for cooking
Ghee	Clarified butter which has a strong flavour; used in Indian cooking
Spreadable	Butter which remains soft in the refrigerator because it has had vegetable oil added to it; sold in sealed plastic containers; lower in fat options are available

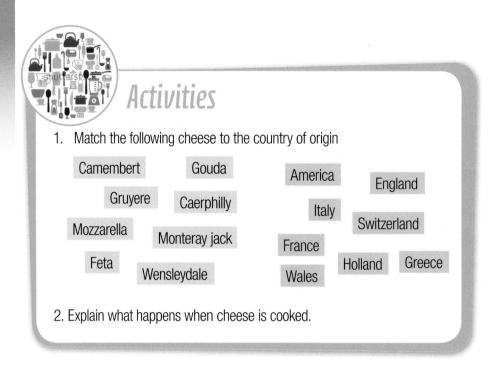

Activities

1. Match the following cheese to the country of origin

Camembert   Gouda   America   England

Gruyere   Caerphilly   Italy   Switzerland

Mozzarella   Monteray jack   France

Feta   Wensleydale   Wales   Holland   Greece

2. Explain what happens when cheese is cooked.

3.5 Eggs

Most of the eggs we eat in the UK come from hens but duck, goose and quail eggs are also available. It is estimated that we eat about 170 eggs each a year.

Hens' eggs are farmed in different ways:

- Free range eggs – where the hens are allowed open air and free runs.
- Barn eggs – where the hens are kept in large sheds and can move around freely.
- Battery eggs – where the hens are kept in cages and never see daylight.

Organic eggs are from hens which live on organic land and are fed on an organic diet.

The inside of an egg

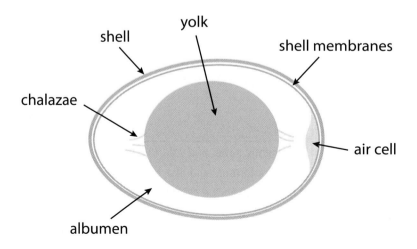

Nutritional value of eggs

Eggs are a nutritious food because they contain most of the nutrients we need. They are an excellent source of protein, rich in vitamin A, D and E in the yolk and B vitamins in the white. Eggs contain calcium (white) and iron (yolk) as well as some zinc. There is a little fat in the yolk and water mainly in the egg white. A medium-sized egg contains 90 kcal (336kJ).

Functions of eggs in cooking

Eggs can be cooked in different ways and eaten on their own or with other foods. Examples are boiling, frying, poaching, making into omelettes and scrambled egg. They also have different uses in many recipes.

Function (use)	Description	Examples
Trapping air (aerating)	Egg protein can stretch as it is whisked or beaten. Air becomes trapped within the eggs, and this makes mixtures light and foamy. It can also help cakes to rise.	Mousses, cold soufflés sponges, meringues (where egg white only is used)
Binding	Eggs stick ingredients together and become solid (**coagulate**) when heated.	Fish cakes, burgers, stuffing, rissoles
Coating	Foods which are fried are coated in raw egg before dipping in crumbs or flour. The egg protein coagulates on heating, seals the food as it cooks and forms a crispy coating.	Fish in batter, scotch eggs, fish cakes
Glazing	Beaten egg is brushed on the surface of dishes to give a shine and brown colour.	Savoury pastry dishes, bread, scones
Emulsifying	The egg yolk contains lecithin, which holds together oil and water and stops them from separating.	Mayonnaise
Thickening	Egg protein coagulates on heating and causes thickening.	Sauces, custards
Enriching	Adding egg to a dish makes it richer in nutrients.	Sauces, custards, mashed potato, milk puddings, pasta
Garnish	Sliced boiled egg is used to give colour to a dish.	Salads

Examples of dishes illustrating different functions of egg:

Quiche

Scotch eggs

Key terms

Coagulation – to become solid or to set.

Glazing – brushing egg or egg and milk on top of baked goods before baking to create a shine and a browned appearance.

Emulsification – when a substance prevents ingredients from separating.

Garnish – a decoration on a savoury dish.

Lion quality mark – eggs have been produced to a high standard. Hens tested for Salmonella bacteria.

Cross-contamination – when bacteria cross from one food to another.

Lemon meringue pie

Fish cakes

Egg salad

Swiss roll

Buying eggs

When cooking with eggs, it is useful to know the size grading:

- Very large – weight of 73g or more.
- Large – weight of 63–73g.
- Medium – weight of 53–63g.
- Small – 53g or less.

Labelling information on an egg box:

Lion quality mark

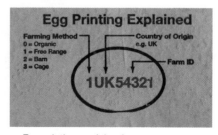
Egg printing explained

Safety

Eggs need to be handled and stored correctly because raw egg contains bacteria. It is therefore important to wash your hands before and after handling raw eggs otherwise **cross-contamination** can occur. Eggs should be stored away from strong-smelling foods because the shell is porous and absorbs smell. They should be kept at a temperature below 20°C.

Activities

1. Explain the function of eggs when making:
   a) A Swiss roll (whisked mixture).
   b) A quiche.
   c) Scotch eggs.
2. a) List the information found on an egg box.
   b) Evaluate the usefulness of this information.

Stretch and challenge

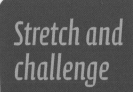

Plan a two-course meal where eggs are a main ingredient in the main course. Give reasons for your choice of dishes.

Check your understanding

1. What is the nutritive value of eggs?
2. Describe the type of eggs available to the consumer in the UK.

3.6 Fruits and vegetables

Fruits and vegetables are important in our diet. We should eat at least five **portions** every day. The portions can be fresh, frozen, dried fruit or fruit juice and canned vegetables. Potatoes do not count as a portion.

Nutritional value

Fruits and vegetables contain a range of nutrients:

- **Carbohydrate** in the form of natural sugars and starches.
- **Vitamins A, C and E,** which are antioxidant and protect against diseases such as cancers. Citrus fruits and green vegetables are high in vitamin C.
- Red, orange and yellow coloured fruit and vegetables are high in beta carotene, which is made into vitamin A in the body.
- **Protein** in beans, peas and lentils.

> **Key term**
>
> **Portion** – the size and weight of food we eat.

Fruits and vegetables are:

- High in fibre.
- Low in fat.
- Low in calories.

Fruits and vegetables are the edible parts of plants.

Fruits can be grouped together according to type:

- Fruit with stones – apricots, cherries, damsons, greengages, nectarines, peaches, and plums.
- Citrus fruit – clementines, grapefruit, kumquats, lemons, limes, mandarins, pomelo, oranges and tangerines.
- Hard fruits – apples, pears and quinces.
- Soft berry fruits – blackberries, blueberries, bilberries, cranberries, gooseberries, raspberries and strawberries.
- Currants – blackcurrants, redcurrants and whitecurrants.
- Exotic fruit, or those that do not fit into any of the above groups – bananas, dates, passion fruit, figs, grapes, guavas, kiwi fruit, mangoes, melons, lychees, sharon fruit, pineapple and pomegranates.

Berry fruits

Currant fruits

Fruit with stones

Examples of citrus fruits

Different varieties of apples and pears

Examples of exotic fruits

Vegetables can be grouped together according to type.

Those growing under the ground:

- Root vegetables – beetroot, carrots, celeriac, parsnips, radishes, swedes, turnip.
- Tubers – potatoes, sweet potato, Jerusalem artichokes.
- Bulbs – onions, leeks, shallots, garlic.

Root vegetables   *Examples of tubers*   *Examples of bulbs*

Those growing above the ground:

- Leaves – cabbage, Brussels sprouts, lettuce, spinach, watercress, pak choi, kale.
- Flower heads – broccoli, cauliflower.
- Stems – asparagus, celery, rhubarb, chicory.
- Fungi – mushrooms.

Examples of leaves   *Examples of flower heads*   *Examples of stems*

Examples of mushrooms

Some fruits such as tomatoes, avocado pears, aubergines, peppers, sweet corn, marrows, courgettes and butternut squash are eaten as vegetables.

Legume or pulse vegetables such as beans, peas and lentils are really seeds but we use them as vegetables. (See Topic 3.9 on Beans, peas and lentils.)

Runner beans, broad beans and French beans, peas are also used as vegetables.

Legumes

French beans

Peas

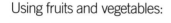

Runner beans

Broad beans

Bean sprouts are a good source of vitamin C; good raw in salads or in stir-fries and Chinese dishes.

Bean sprouts

Using fruits and vegetables:

Fruits	Vegetables
● Raw, with or without skins	● Raw, with or without skin in salads and as side dishes
● Stewed	
● Baked in the oven	● In soups and to flavour stock
● As dried fruit, for example apricots, bananas, raisins, currants, sultanas, currants	● Roasted, baked, fried, stir-fried, barbecued, boiled, steamed, braised and cooked in a microwave
● Canned, bottled in syrup or preserved as jam or chutney	● Canned but the heat process destroys some of the vitamins
● Most fruits freeze well	● Some vegetables can be dried
● Blended and used in smoothies and fruit sauces (called coulis)	● Preserved in vinegar, for example onion, cucumbers and pickles
● Preserved in sugar as crystallised or candied fruit, for example pineapple, cherries, orange and lemon	● As an **accompaniment** in a meal
● Added to jellies and mousses	● In recipes such as risottos, casseroles, coated in a cheese sauce, pasta dishes
● Served with meat, for example pork apple, turkey with cranberry, mango in curries	● Stuffed with fillings, for example peppers, courgettes, jacket potatoes

All fresh fruits and vegetables should be used soon after purchase. The longer they are stored before use, the more the vitamin content is reduced. Store them in a cool place. Bruised or damaged fruits and vegetables will not keep for long; cut off the bruised or damaged part and use straightaway.

Buy fruits and vegetables when they in season and at their best flavour and condition.

Preparation and cooking of fruits and vegetables:

- Peel thinly or leave the peel on if possible as most of the nutrients are found under the skin.
- Prepare just before they are used or cooked. Vitamin C is destroyed by time and heat.
- Do not leave vegetables standing in water, as the nutrients soak into the water.
- Do not chop too small. The larger the surface area, the more nutrients are kept in the fruits and vegetables.
- Cook immediately after preparation.
- Cook vegetables quickly using a very small amount of water. Steaming or microwaving are quick methods and lose fewer vitamins.
- Do not keep cooked vegetables warm for long as the vitamins are lost.

Key terms

Legumes – a plant that has pods as fruit, used as food.

Accompaniment – an item that is added because it goes well with something.

Activity

We are recommended to eat more fruit and vegetables because they contain antioxidants. Find out more about antioxidants and explain why they have health benefits.

Stretch and challenge

1. Research recipes to find interesting ways of including fruits and vegetables in the diet.

2. Design a leaflet which will encourage teenagers to eat more fruits and vegetables.

Check your understanding

1. What is the nutritional value of fruits and vegetables?
2. Discuss the benefits of steaming green vegetables.
3. Describe three examples of how fruits and vegetables can be preserved.

Key terms

Culinary – relating to food or cooking.

Staple foods – form a large part of the diet and are usually starchy foods.

Durum wheat – a special variety of wheat used to make pasta.

Examples of herbs
Basil
Bayleaf
Coriander
Garlic
Mint
Parsley
Rosemary
Sage
Thyme

Examples of spices
Cayenne pepper
Cinnamon
Cloves
Ginger
Mustard
Nutmeg
Paprika
Turmeric
Vanilla

3.7 Herbs and spices

Herbs and spices have influenced multicultural cooking over the years. Many have medicinal uses as well as **culinary** uses.

Herbs are the leaves, stems and roots of plants that are used to flavour foods. When herbs are crushed, chopped or heated, aromatic oils are released which add flavour.

Spices are the dried roots, bark or seeds of plants. They are sold crushed or powdered or as whole seeds. When whole seeds are crushed or heated, they release aromatic flavours.

3.8 Cereals

Cereals are the seeds or grains of plants. Cereals are known as **staple foods**. They contain starch and are therefore good sources of energy. The main cereals used for food products are: barley, maize, oats, rice, rye, spelt, wheat, quinoa.

Nutritional value

Cereals provide protein, carbohydrate, dietary fibre, B vitamins and some iron. Some types contain a little fat.

The best way to eat cereals, if possible, is as wholegrain or wholemeal. Wholemeal or wholegrain means unprocessed or unrefined, that is, in its most natural state. Many cereals are processed or refined before we eat them. The most common process is milling the cereal to make flour. You will learn more in Topic 11.3 on Flour on page 110.

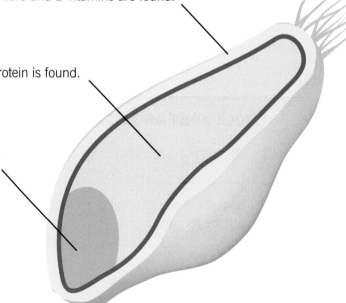

Bran or outer layer.
This is where the fibre and B vitamins are found.

Endosperm or middle part.
This is where the starch and protein is found.

Germ or smallest part.
This is where the new plant grows, and where the fat and B vitamins are found.

A grain of wheat

Types of cereals

The chart tells you what each cereal is used for and whether it contains gluten. This information is important for successful bread making and for someone who has coeliac disease. (See Topic 2.8 on Food intolerance on pages 51–53.)

Name of cereal	What it is used for
Barley *contains gluten*	• made into flour • bread • pearl barley used in soups • making beer and whisky • barley flakes used in breakfast cereals • malt extract made from barley, used for cooking and as a sweetener
Maize *no gluten*	• milled into cornflour • cornmeal (polenta) used to make bread, biscuits, cakes, muffins • corn oil • corn on the cob • dried maize used for popcorn • breakfast cereals
Oats *a little gluten*	• sold as oatmeal, porridge oats, jumbo oat flakes • made into oatcakes, flapjacks oat biscuits
Rice *no gluten*	• many varieties available: short grain and long grain • short grain – for making puddings and sweet dishes • long grain such as patna, basmati, easy cook – for curries, paella and other savoury dishes • made into flour • rice flakes used in breakfast cereals
Rye *some gluten*	• made into flour • bread • rye flakes added to breakfast cereals
Spelt *some gluten*	• made into flour • used to make bread
Wheat *contains gluten*	• made into different types of flour • bulgar wheat is steamed whole wheat grains • couscous is steamed, dried and cracked grains of **durum wheat** • wheat flakes used in breakfast cereals • wheat germ can be bought and added to recipes, rich in vitamin E • wheat bran can be bought and added to recipes • semolina is a wheat product, used for puddings, and added to cakes and biscuit recipes
Quinoa *no gluten*	• used instead of rice in some recipes • very high in protein

Pasta is made from durum wheat, which is a variety of strong flour high in gluten. Pasta is made by mixing flour, water or egg to make a paste and it is then formed into different shapes. Pasta is a good source of carbohydrate and contains some protein and fibre, B vitamins. Wholemeal (brown) pasta has more fibre than white pasta.

Activities

1. What is meant by 'refined' and 'unrefined' cereals?

2. Carry out research into breakfast cereals. Record your findings in a table listing each cereal and the breakfast cereals made from the cereal.

Check your understanding

1. What are cereals?

2. Name three uses for each of the following cereals:

   a) Wheat

   b) Maize

   c) Rice

3. What are the main nutrients in cereals?

3.9 Legumes, nuts and seeds

Legumes are also known as pulses. They include beans, lentils and peas.

Nutritional value of pulses

Pulses are low in fat, good sources of protein, fibre, vitamins and minerals. They contain some carbohydrate, B vitamins and some iron.

Different peas, beans and lentils

Key term

Legumes – also known as pulses.

Brown flax seeds	Sunflower seeds	Peanuts	Poppy seeds
Pistachios	Almonds	Sesame seeds	Walnuts
Hazelnuts	Pine nuts	Wheat germ	Ground flax seeds
Golden flax seeds	Brazil nut	Cashew nuts	Pumpkin seeds

Seeds and nuts

Pulses are available dried, frozen and in cans. Dried pulses need to be soaked in water before cooking. Some, such as kidney beans, need to be soaked for 12 hours and boiled for 15 minutes to destroy the toxin in the skins. Canned kidney beans are safe to use straight from the tin.

Some of the most popular pulses are: peas, chick peas, lentils and soya beans. Soya beans have many uses. They are made into soya milk, tofu, TVP (see next page) and soya sauce. Soya is a high biological value protein and is widely used in vegan diets to supply essential amino acids.

Mung beans and bean sprouts are widely used in salads because they are excellent sources of vitamin C.

Mung beans which grow into bean sprouts when they have germinated

Nutritional value of nuts and seeds

Nuts provide protein and vitamins A and E, potassium and phosphorus. They contain fibre and carbohydrates and are high in fat.

Peanuts are very high in protein. They are made into peanut butter.

Seeds are a good source of protein. They can be added to salads, used in biscuit and bread recipes to add flavour, texture and nutritive value.

3.10 Alternative protein foods

Soya protein

Soya protein is made from soya beans and used in many food products. Soya beans are a high biological value protein food.

Soya beans are made into: soya flour which can be used to make bread and textured vegetable protein products (TVP). TVP is widely used in vegetarian products: it can be manufactured into different shapes and flavoured to give the taste and texture of meat or chicken. Granose soya mince is made from 100% dried soya and only needs to have water added before it is ready for use in cooking.

Tofu

Tofu is soya bean curd made by setting soya milk with calcium sulphate. Tofu is soft and creamy in texture and can be cut into chunks to use in stir-fries. Tofu is a very good source of protein and is low in fat.

Tofu

Quorn products

Quorn

Quorn is a mycoprotein made artificially and mixed with egg white and flavourings. It is processed into different shapes and textures and made into burgers, sausages, fillets, which can be used for meals. Quorn has a high amount of high biological value protein and all the B vitamins except B12. It is low in fat.

TVP, available as mince, chunks, flavoured or unflavoured

Activities

1. Explain why soya beans are widely used in a vegan diet.

2. Research a Quorn product such as beef mince on the Internet.

   Find out the cost and nutritional values and compare with fresh beef mince.

   Comment on your findings.

Check your understanding

1. Name some of the products that are made from soya beans.
2. Why do you think people other than vegans and vegetarians are choosing to buy meat alternatives?

Exam practice

1. There is a variety of fish available to the consumer.

   a) Identify the different types of fish available to the consumer. [6]

   b) Discuss ways of promoting fish by making interesting fish dishes. [6]

2. State three nutrients found in milk. [3]

3. Supermarkets sell a wide range of different milks. Discuss the reasons why such a wide range is now available. [6]

4. Eggs have many uses in food preparation. Explain, with examples, the different uses of eggs when making food products. [8]

5. Suggest ways of reducing the loss of vitamins when cooking green vegetables. [4]

6. a) Name two salads that could be offered for sale in the school canteen. [2]

   b) Explain why salad dressings are used with salads. [3]

Topic 4: Factors affecting consumer choice

What will I learn?

- **Information about different foods.**
- **Factors that influence our decisions on what to eat.**

Why do we choose to eat the foods that we do?

There is plenty of choice available, and, sometimes we take this for granted. However, food choice can be influenced by many factors:

- Availability – climate, whether food is grown locally or imported and the food shops that are available to us.
- Acceptability – culture, religious rules and traditions, personal beliefs and values, likes and dislikes, personal needs all have an influence on food choice.
- Affordability – the rising cost of food, whether we make our own or buy ready-made.

4.1 Cost

Cost is one of the most important factors that influence choice of food. Some people think eating healthily is expensive but this is not necessarily the case. The amount people spend on food varies according to the amount of money which comes into the home.

Many people on a limited budget struggle to pay for basic things such as paying the rent or mortgage, heating and lighting bills, clothing, transport and food. They may have to cut down on the amount they spend on food, which may mean buying cheaper products which often contain high amounts of sugar and fat, and are often highly processed foods.

There are ways in which we can save money and make good choices to provide **nutritious** meals even if we are on a limited budget:

- Planning meals is always a good starting point. Try to think of recipes where you can double up on ingredients, e.g. if you buy leeks you could use half to make a leek and potato soup and the other half to use in a casserole. Make a shopping list of everything you need and avoid buying on impulse.
- Take advantage of 'special offers' in the shops, e.g. buy-one-get-one-free, but do not buy more than you need or can use.
- Compare food prices on an Internet site such as mySupermarket.com.
- Buy cheaper cuts of meat and offal, e.g. shin of beef, belly pork, liver or heart.
- Add cheaper sources of protein such as beans and pulses to meat in a recipe. This can make the dish cheaper because they 'bulk up' and make the meat go further.

- Buy **seasonal** foods which are always cheaper at the particular time of year when they are plentiful and are a lot tastier.
- Collect and use supermarket vouchers, coupons, loyalty points.
- Buy supermarket own brands or value lines, which are often cheaper than other brands.
- Avoid waste – don't buy more than you need and eat food before the 'use by' date.
- Use up left over food creatively. Left over mashed potato, for example, can be used as a topping for a cottage pie or used to make fish cakes.
- Particular methods of cooking and cooking equipment use less fuel than others. Microwaves and slow cookers, for example, use less electricity for cooking food than using a conventional cooker.
- When cooking, double up on recipes. Use half and freeze the other half for a later date.

What else do we need to think about?

- In the UK we are constantly being reminded that we need look after the environment and prevent waste. We produce just over half of our food needs, the rest is brought in from other countries. Evidence suggests that by using good farming techniques we could increase what we produce in this country to feed the population and be more **sustainable**.
- We can reduce food waste. We waste more than £10 billion worth in the UK each year. Some food waste goes to landfill but many local authorities operate weekly collections and the waste is composted. We can also help at home by turning waste food into compost.
- Food is a basic need. Global food prices are on the increase. The challenge in the 21st century is to produce more food with fewer resources such as land, water and fuel, to feed a growing global population.
- Over one billion people worldwide are overweight or obese.
- Over one billion people do not have access to enough food.
- An additional one billion people have inadequate **micronutrient** intakes.

Key terms

Nutritious – containing the substances in food that aid good health.

Seasonal – available or grown only at particular times of the year.

Sustainable – being able to keep something going for a long time.

Micronutrient – needed in small amounts, these are the vitamins and minerals.

Activities

1. Two students are sharing a flat and have a limited amount of money to spend on food each week. They like to prepare and cook their own evening meals from scratch. Plan a week's evening meals for the students that will be low cost, interesting and nutritious.

   Give reasons for your choice.

2. How do you think supermarkets can help people on low incomes to get good value for their money when buying food?

Check your understanding

1. How can people save money when:
   a) Buying food for family meals?
   b) Cooking meals at home?

4.2 Culture

Culture is a word used to describe a way of life which makes us different from other people. It influences beliefs, laws, morals, customs and often religion. Culture is learned from the time we are born. We are often not aware of the influence it has on what, when and how we eat.

Examples of food culture include:

- Which foods are acceptable to eat and which are not.
- Which foods are considered good and which are considered bad for you.
- What is an acceptable way to eat food and what is not an acceptable way.

4.3 Religion

Many religions have laws and rules which limit their food choices and forbid eating certain foods. These rules are often linked to celebrations, traditions or times of the year.

The table lists some of the main religions and the rules that link to their food choice:

Religious faith	Food choice or dietary rules
Buddhism	• Many are vegetarians, as their religion preaches against killing. • Some avoid meat and dairy products. • Fasting is practised by the Buddhist monks in the afternoon.
Christianity	• No food is forbidden. • Many Christians observe Lent, when they give up certain foods for 40 days and 40 nights. • On Good Friday some may avoid eating meat. • Traditional food, such as turkey and mince pies, is eaten at Christmas.
Hinduism	• Eating beef is forbidden, some do not eat pork. • Foods like onions, garlic, mushrooms, tea and coffee are avoided by strict Hindus. • Alcohol is forbidden and many Hindus eat vegetarian diets.
Islam	• Food choice is based on the Holy Book, the Qur'an which sets out rules forbidding meat and poultry unless it is slaughtered the halal (lawful) Islamic way. • The following foods are not allowed: pork, pork products, gelatine, alcohol, products containing animal fats, frozen vegetables, some types of margarine, drinks containing caffeine and breads containing dried yeast.
Judaism	• Food must be kosher, which means that it must be 'clean'. • Pork and shell fish are forbidden, all meat and poultry must be slaughtered in a special way to be kosher and meat and dairy produce must not be prepared or eaten together. • Fasting is part of Judaism, on the day of Atonement, they fast from dusk till dusk. • Jewish feast days include Rosh Hashanah and the Passover when bitter herbs are eaten to remind Jews of the suffering of the Israelites under Egyptian rule.
Rastafarianism	• Foods must be natural and clean. • Some are vegans or vegetarians and use coconut oil to cook food. They do not eat pork or fish longer than 30cm long. • They do not drink alcohol, coffee or milk.

4.4 Ethics

People are concerned about **factory farming**, **global warming**, **fair trading** and **environmental issues**. This could influence where people choose to buy their food and their food choice.

Farmers' markets sell locally produced food, mainly fruit, vegetables, meat, cheese, eggs, bread, cakes, pickles and chutneys. The foods sold must come from the local area and the products must contain local ingredients. These foods can also be sold in farm shops and box schemes and are regulated by the National Farmers' Retail Markets Association.

Fair trade products aim to give farmers in developing countries a better deal. The Fair Trade Foundation ensures that farmers get a fair price for their produce, enough to give them a steady income. Fair trade products include coffee, sugar, tea, chocolate.

Another concern is the distance food travels before it gets to us, 'from field to plate' called **food miles**. Food miles make us aware of the effect transporting food around the world has on our environment. Some foods travel a great distance by sea, air and road to arrive in the UK to give consumers a wider choice.

Many foods, such as fruit and vegetables, can only be grown in this country at particular times of the year or in greenhouses which need to be heated. It is considered to be cheaper to import many fruit and vegetables, particularly during the winter, because of these costs.

Key terms

Factory farming – a farm where animals are reared in large quantities.

Global warming – an increase in the world's temperatures, believed to be caused by the greenhouse effect.

Fair trade – to help producers get a fair price for their produce, to help with working conditions.

Environmental issues – relating to our surroundings and the world around us.

4.5 Organic foods

Organic food is produced as naturally as possible, without the use of artificial chemical fertilisers or pesticides. Farmers are allowed to use about four of the many hundreds of pesticides available under special circumstances but their use is strictly controlled.

Organically produced animals are reared naturally without the use of medication or drugs and must have access to outdoor, organic land. Numbers of animals produced must be controlled, allowing animals plenty of room and freedom to move around.

In the UK the Soil Association or Organic Farmers and Growers are the main organisations which make checks on farms and produce to make sure that these strict standards are met.

Why choose organic?

The sale of organic food and the range of organic produce have increased over recent years. Organic foods are available in supermarkets, farmers' markets, farm shops and by mail order. Some companies operate organic box schemes where you pay for the delivery of organic fruit and vegetables or collect orders from a 'drop off' point.

Organic produce is more nutritious and thought to contain more vitamins and minerals than non-organic produce. It tastes better as the food is grown naturally and has not travelled far. Organic food saves on **carbon footprints**.

Many people are concerned over the use of pesticides on and the additives used in non-organic food because of the possible long-term effects these may have on our health.

There is also concern over animal welfare, **intensive farming** and the effects on the environment. Organic farming is more sustainable and is less harmful to our planet than intensive farming methods.

Logos on food packaging which help us make ethical choices:

4.6 Genetically modified foods

Genetically modified (GM) foods are a relatively new and complex form of science. Genes from plants or animals can be transferred in ways that were not possible before. Genes from a particular plant are taken and planted in another plant to give that plant a specific, desirable characteristic.

These specific characteristics can make the plant more nutritious, resistant to pests, drought or disease, grow faster or increase shelf life. A chosen plant may produce bigger seeds or deeper coloured fruit or an animal may produce bigger offspring.

Many people are concerned about the use of GM foods for the following reasons:
- Possible health risks and allergic reactions.
- Pollen from GM crops can escape and mix with wild plants and non-GM crops.
- Tampering or playing with nature.
- New resistant micro-organisms could develop which we know little about.

It is not possible to tell by looking which food is GM and which is not. The only way of telling is when the manufacturer puts this information on the label. This information is not always clear on a food label.

When first introduced there was pressure from consumers to stop supermarkets from selling GM foods. These foods included soya beans, sweet corn, sugar beet and sugar cane, rapeseed, tomatoes, kiwi fruit and some types of rice. New GM products include GM maize grown in the USA and GM soya with fish oils.

There are no GM crops currently being grown commercially in the UK.

4.7 Functional foods

Functional foods are foods which contain naturally occurring substances which can have a positive effect on health and well-being or lower the risk of developing certain diseases. They should not, however, be seen as an alternative to a varied and well-balanced diet and a healthy lifestyle. Legislation exists to protect the consumer from misleading claims about the possible benefits on health.

Examples of functional foods are **probiotic** drinks and yogurts, cholesterol-lowering spreads and some types of bread.

Functional food	Suggested health benefit
Foods made from soya beans	Lower cholesterol levels; reduce risk of developing heart disease
Margarine made with plant stanols and sterol esters, e.g. Benecol	Lower cholesterol levels
Whole oat products	Reduce risk of heart disease and lower cholesterol levels
Green tea	Reduce risk of developing some types of cancers
Oily fish containing omega-3 fatty acids	Reduce risk of heart disease
Probiotics	Good effect on the intestines and immune system
Garlic	Lower blood cholesterol levels

Probiotic bread

> ## Key terms
>
> **Functional foods** – foods that claim to have health benefits.
>
> **Probiotics** – live micro-organisms which may have health benefits in the digestive system.

4.8 Fortified foods

These are foods which have extra nutrients added to them with the aim of improving people's health. Some foods are fortified by law, e.g. margarine; others are fortified voluntarily, e.g. breakfast cereals.

Safety considerations are taken into account when deciding which foods to fortify.

Fortified foods make an important contribution to diets in the UK. Examples are:

- Calcium added voluntarily to soya-based drinks.
- Iron, thiamine and niacin added by law to white and brown flour.
- Vitamin A and D are added by law to margarine.

Breakfast cereals fortified with vitamins and minerals

Eggs fortified with omega 3

Why fortify foods?

Adding nutrients to **staple foods** such as bread, margarine, breakfast cereals, which the majority of the population eat, means people can get a good supply of particular nutrients.

Activity

Make a list of products that are advertised as being rich in a particular nutrient or advertised as probiotic. At whom do you think these products are targeted?

Comment on price, the packaging and other ingredients in the product.

Check your understanding

1. What do the following terms mean:
   a) Organic?
   b) Sustainable?
   c) Genetically modified?
   d) Food miles?
2. Why do people choose to buy organic foods?
3. Explain why ethical issues would influence people's food choice.
4. What are people's main concerns about GM food?

Exam practice

1. The increasing cost of food is encouraging people to find ways of saving money.

   Discuss this in relation to:
   a) The preparation and cooking of food in the home. [6]
   b) Shopping for food. [6]

2. Fortified foods are marketed for their health benefits.

   a) What is a 'fortified food'? [2]

   b) Discuss the range of fortified foods available to the consumer and evaluate the manufacturers' claims. [6]

Topic 5: Marketing and advertising

What will I learn?
- **How food manufacturers attract customers to buy their food.**

The food industry spends an enormous amount of money on marketing and advertising so that they sell their products to make a profit. Marketing is a method used by companies to help sell their products.

Food companies use research methods to find out **consumer** needs in order to provide them with a suitable product. Research includes finding out what other rival food companies produce and identifying target groups in society who are likely to buy the product.

Research methods include:

- Primary research – questionnaires, telephoning, tasting sessions and asking opinions.
- Secondary research – using existing information found on websites and reports.

Product development

Food companies will make a new product and test it on consumers. They also improve existing products or introduce new flavours to add to an existing range of products.

Advertising

Advertising provides the consumer with information about a product or a service. Advertising should give the consumer a reason for buying the product or using the service. Advertising will target the group or groups of people most likely to buy the product or use the service.

The biggest spenders on food and drink advertisements are supermarkets and manufacturers of chocolate, crisps, snacks and sweets. They are clever at creating ways of attracting children to their products. Children have a huge influence on families in decisions over choice of food. This is known as '**pester power**'.

Supermarkets are well known for using different marketing techniques (promotions) to tempt and persuade consumers to buy their products. These include:

- Special introductory price on a 'new product'
- Buy one get one free (bogof)
- Free samples
- Money off vouchers
- % extra
- Gifts with the product

> ## Key terms
>
> **Consumers** – people who buy and use things.
>
> **Pester power** – children's ability to nag and persuade their parents to buy something that they would not otherwise buy.

- Competitions to enter.

Other ways of advertising include:

- Television
- Leaflets and magazines in store
- In magazines, newspapers or delivered to the door
- Posters
- In cinemas and other public places
- On the Internet
- Using celebrities to promote products.

There are strict rules covering advertising. It is the job of the Advertising Standards Authority (ASA) to look into complaints and control advertising. Adverts should be legal, decent, honest and truthful. There are strict rules covering advertising on television and radio to children of foods high in fats, salt and sugar.

Activity

What are the advantages and disadvantages of the following methods of food promotion?

a) Money off vouchers
b) % extra
c) Buy one get one free
d) Free gift with product.

Stretch and challenge

1. Discuss ways in which supermarkets could try to increase the sales of a new range of 'healthier option' foods.

2. Collect a variety of advertisements for food from magazines and newspapers. Which are the most popular and why?

Check your understanding

Make a list of the different ways of advertising a food product.

Exam practice

People are encouraged to make better food choices in order to improve health.

Assess the way in which healthy eating is promoted with reference to:

a) Current campaigns.
b) Supermarket advertising.

Topic 6: Shopping for food

- Types of shops that sell food.
- Shopping habits.

There are many issues that influence what foods people buy and where they buy the foods. These include:

- Price of the food.
- Brand or name of a particular food product.
- Reputation or quality of the food product.
- The amount of time available to spend on shopping for food.
- The choice of shops in the area.
- The reputation of a supermarket, shop or market.

The **Living Costs and Food Survey** shows the following trends:

- We are buying more healthy foods such as fruit and vegetables, fish and high fibre breakfast cereals.
- Our diet is still too high in fatty, salty and sugary foods.
- We spend too much money on eating out compared with buying food to cook at home.

General trends which affect food and shopping:

- There is an increase in one parent families, single people living alone and people living longer.
- Homes are smaller with less space for food storage, preparation and cooking.
- More families are using smaller freezers and refrigerators.
- The microwave is a popular method of cooking or reheating ready prepared meals. The choice in ready meals, frozen dinners and takeaway foods has increased.
- There is a wide interest in popular television cookery programmes which encourage people to cook from scratch.
- Men, women and children often share the task of cooking meals.
- Shift work and activities by family members mean that families are less likely to eat a meal together.
- There is a wide variety of popular, takeaway fast food available.
- People tend to eat more snacks and less sit down type meals.
- People are more aware of 'food miles' (where food has travelled a long distance from its source to the shop).
- Bar coding of food has reduced time spent queuing or paying at the check-out.
- The range of packaging material has increased and improved so that food lasts longer.

Key term

Living Costs and Food Survey – the government survey that finds out what foods we are eating and the trends in our eating habits.

Shopping online:

Advantages
• Order in the comfort of your home
• Goods delivered
• Saves time
• Saves transport costs
• Can compare costs on different websites
• Regular items on your shopping list are saved
• Helps people with mobility difficulties

Disadvantages
• Charge for delivery
• Cannot see the quality of the food
• Sometimes the item is not in stock

 Activity

Find out about the types of food shops in your area. Give examples under the following headings:

- Supermarkets
- Small shops
- Farmers' markets or other markets
- Specialist shops or delicatessens.

Shopping for food:

- Supermarkets supply a wide range of foods and other goods. This means that consumers can buy everything they need under one roof.
- Many individual shops such as bakers, butchers, fishmongers, greengrocers and delicatessens have closed in town centres. However, they have increased in smaller towns as a result of campaigning and interest in food programmes on television.
- Many corner shops in towns and cities stock a range of food items and are useful for people who do not want to travel far to buy food.
- People who are working tend to do a weekly or monthly shop from supermarkets.
- Online ordering of food from supermarkets is a popular option. The food is delivered to the door, which saves time.
- Farmers' markets and street markets are popular with people who like to support local produce and buy fresh organic foods.
- Mail order companies, selling a variety of foods, will pack and send food to your home.

Why have trends in food and shopping for food changed?

- More women work outside the home.
- Busier lifestyles.
- More people own cars and can drive to the larger food stores on the outskirts of towns and cities.
- Foreign travel is popular; people try out new foods in other countries.
- Advances in technology make it possible to choose and buy at home.
- The influence of advertising and television programmes has encouraged people to try new foods.
- People do not have the skills to prepare and cook food from scratch at home. Can't cook, won't cook?

 Check your understanding

1. List the advantages and disadvantages of shopping for food online.

2. Explain how shopping trends have changed over the years. Give reasons why these changes have taken place.

Exam practice

People are influenced by a number of ethical issues when they buy food. Discuss some of these issues.

Topic 7: Food packaging

What will I learn?

- Why and how food is packaged.
- How packaging creates waste and rubbish.

Packaging protects food, keeps it safe and fresh for a longer time. Labels on packaging carry information, some of which is required by law.

The main purposes of food packaging are:

- To preserve the product.
- To protect the product from damage.
- To make the product more attractive to the consumer.
- To make it easier to transport the product.

Packaging materials

Paper, card, metal, plastic and glass can be used for packaging:

Material	Advantages	Disadvantages
Paper and card	Easy to print on, cheap to produce, biodegradable, recyclable, can be moulded, can be coated, lightweight	Water-resistant, easily damaged
Plastic	Versatile – plastics can be flexible or rigid; can be made into shapes, resistant to acids and other chemicals, easy to print on, lightweight and fairly cheap to make	A litter problem, does not biodegrade easily
Metal	Recyclable, lightweight, good barrier to water and gas, can be printed on easily	May react with food
Glass	Reusable, heat resistant, recyclable, keeps its shape, low cost	Breaks easily, heavy, safety issues

Uses:

Paper and board – cartons, paper bags, juice cartons, egg boxes

Plastic – bottles, trays, squeezy bottles

Metal – cans, foil trays, foil tops

Glass – jars and bottles, baby food

Modified atmosphere packaging (MAP)

Food manufacturers can change the type of gas inside packaging to increase the shelf life of the product and to slow down loss of colour. MAP replaces most of the oxygen inside the pack with carbon dioxide and nitrogen. MAP is used to package: cold meats, smoked fish, bacon, minced meat, ready prepared salads and fresh pasta.

Vacuum packing

All the air is removed from inside the pack leaving the food with no oxygen. Without oxygen, the food keeps fresh for longer unopened.

Tamper-proof packaging

Shows that the pack has not been opened and the contents have not been changed or damaged. Examples are shrink-wrapped jars, plastic collars on bottles and pop up on lids of jars. See examples below:

Environmentally friendly packaging

Environmentally friendly packaging causes less damage to the environment. There are three main types:

- Reusable – can be cleaned and reused, for example glass jars.
- Recyclable – made of materials that can be used again usually after processing, for example glass, metal, card and paper.
- Biodegradable – will easily break down in the soil or in the atmosphere. Food manufacturers are increasingly using more biodegradable packaging.

Recycling

Recycling is good for the environment. In June 2010 Wales became the first country within the UK to make recycling a legal requirement. Recycling and the composting of waste food is an attempt by some local authorities to become a zero waste nation by 2050. Homes are being encouraged to sort waste for collection of waste food and recycling of glass, cardboard and paper, cans and plastic.

We waste a great deal of food in the UK each year. Most of it goes to landfill. One fifth of our carbon emissions are created by the production, processing, transport and storage of food. We need to waste less food to become more environmentally friendly. Many local authorities are collecting waste food and using a **biodigester** to turn the waste food into electricity and fertiliser.

Every year UK households throw away the equivalent of 3½ million double-decker buses (almost 30 million tonnes), a queue of which would stretch from London to Sydney (Australia) and back.

Key terms

Environmentally friendly – to minimise harm to the natural world, e.g. by using biodegradable ingredients.

Biodigester – a method of processing waste food to produce electricity or fertiliser.

Typical contents of a household bin

35% Organic

30% Paper

12% Construction

9% Plastics

6% Metal

5% Other

3% Glass

International recycling symbol

Tidy man symbol encouraging consumers to throw rubbish in the bin

Aluminium cans can be recycled

Manufacturers and consumers are being encouraged to use less packaging. Shoppers should use only what is essential, reuse containers and recycle as much as possible.

Reduce: buy less packaged food and avoid foods which are overpackaged. Avoid taking too many plastic bags when packing food shopping.

Reuse: buy refillable products such as cleaning liquids whenever possible. Reuse plastic bags and glass jars.

Recycle: many materials such as paper, glass, paper and plastic can be collected or taken to banks for recycling.

Check your understanding

1. List the main food packaging materials. State the advantages and disadvantages of each.
2. Give reasons why food is packaged.

Exam practice

Food packaging is changing in order to reduce the effects on the environment.

a) Discuss why food packaging is required by the food industry. [6]

b) Evaluate how food packaging has been developed in order to reduce the impact on the environment. [6]

Activity

1. Describe modified atmosphere packaging.
2. What is meant by biodegradable packaging?
3. What is tamper-proof packaging? Give two examples of its use.

Topic 8: Food labelling

Key terms

Best before date – the quality of the food is not as good after that date.

Use by date – the food will go off, so it must be used before that date.

A food label can provide information which is useful to the consumer. In addition to the information, food labels attract customers by being colourful and attractive. Food manufacturers know this and spend a lot of time and money designing packaging and labels in order to tempt consumers to buy their product.

The Food Labelling Regulations of 1996 require certain information to be given on all pre-packed foods. These requirements are written by the European Union (EU). These are the items on the label that are required by law:

- Manufacturer's name and contact details
- Name of the product
- Description of the product
- Weight (some foods are exempt, for example bread)
- Ingredients (listed in descending order of weight, i.e. largest amount first)
- Cooking/heating instructions
- Storage instructions
- Shelf life – **best before** and **use by dates**
- Place of origin
- Allergy information.

The following items are not legal requirements, but are nevertheless good practice and often included on packaging:

- Illustration of product
- Price
- Nutritional values of the product
- Customer guarantee
- The batch-code and bar-code numbers
- Opening instructions.

Nutritional information

This is compulsory only if the food has a special claim, for example 'low in fat', 'high in fibre' or 'reduced salt'.

There are guidelines on giving nutritional information. The nutrients should be given per 100g or 100ml amounts of a food. Some values are also given per portion. The information should either be set out in a table or written as a list:

- Energy as kJ and kcal
- Protein in grams (g)

- Carbohydrate in grams of which sugars should be shown in grams
- Fat in grams of which saturates should be shown in grams
- Fibre in grams
- Sodium in grams.

Other nutrients such as vitamins, minerals, starch and sugars can be shown but must be shown if a claim is made about them.

Quantitative Ingredient Declaration (QUID)

The quantity of an ingredient used in a food product is shown as a percentage. This information is useful when comparing products.

Example:

Chicken and ham pie – filling 52%, pastry 46%
Chicken and ham pie (economy) – filling 44%, pastry 54%
Chicken and ham pie (luxury) – filling 58%, pastry 40%

Guideline daily amounts

Guideline daily amounts (GDA) are guidelines for healthy adults. They help plan a healthy, balanced diet and a GDA label has five parts: calories, sugars, fat, saturates and salt.

*A label with **GDA and traffic light** information*

Traffic lights system

The Food Standards Agency has tried to make nutritional information on food labels easier to understand by introducing the traffic lights system. The three colours – red, orange and green show if the food is high, medium or low in fat, saturated fat, sugars and salt.

Allergy information

There are particular foods or ingredients that people may be allergic to, and, when present, these have to be listed on the packaging, usually in a box labeled 'allergy advice'. The foods are: celery, cereals containing gluten, crustaceans (including prawns, crabs and lobsters), eggs, fish, lupin, milk, molluscs (mussels and oysters), mustard, nuts, peanuts, sesame seeds, soya beans, sulphur dioxide and sulphites.

Other information

Special dietary needs. Labels show if the product: is suitable for vegetarians, is gluten free, contains peanuts.

Symbols for recycling:

Gluten free symbol

Recycling logo

International symbol reminding people not to drop litter

Indicates the oven is
a microwave oven

Power output

800W

F

Heating category

*Microwave symbol showing that food
can be cooked in a microwave oven
and what power*

*Red Tractor logo, a guarantee to
consumers that the food has been
produced to high standards of food
safety and hygiene and animal
welfare*

*Freedom Food symbol, showing that
the food has been produced to high
animal welfare standards*

Why is food labelling information important?

- To help consumers make an informed choice and make their own decisions whether to buy the product.
- To help consumers make decisions about value for money.
- To give consumers who have health conditions information about the fat, sugar, salt or fibre content.
- People who have allergies need to know if the food is safe for them to eat.
- The name and address of the manufacturer is there if a consumer has a complaint about the food.
- Storage, heating and cooking instructions are there for consumers.
- Consumers who need to avoid certain foods or ingredients for religious or cultural reasons.
- Consumers who have strong views and concerns about animal welfare and environmental issues can make decisions.

Activity

Look at the food label for Crunchy Nut Cornflakes on page 100.

a) In a 50g portion, what will it provide of the following:
  - Kcalories?
  - Protein?
  - Sugars?
  - Sodium?

b) List other information on the label.

c) Explain why this information is useful to the consumer.

Check your understanding

1. Explain what is meant by:
   a) Use by date?
   b) Bar codes?

2. Describe the traffic light system and explain why it is useful on a food label.

Topic 9: New food developments

Traditional biotechnology mainly involves the production of foods such as cheese, bread and wine.

9.1 Nanotechnology

Nanotechnology is the manufacture and use of materials and structures at the nanometre scale (a nanometre is one millionth of a millimetre). It offers a wide range of opportunities for the development of new products and for food packaging.

The texture of food can be changed as food spreadability and stability (not changing) improve with nano-sized crystals and liquids for better low fat foods.

The flavour of a food can be changed with bitter blockers or sweet and salty **enhancers**.

Nano-enhanced bacteria keep oxygen-sensitive foods fresher.

Modified starch is used to improve mouth-feel, thicken the drink with the addition of boiled water, and blend with no lumps

9.2 Smart foods

Smart foods (sometimes known as modern/novel materials/foods) is a collective term for the study of new developments in materials. Smart materials are:

• Developed through the invention of new or improved processes.
• Altered to perform a particular function.
• Developed for specialised applications.

What are smart foods?
Examples are:

• Modified starch (e.g. instant dessert mix that uses cold milk to thicken without heating).
• Genetically modified foods.
• Antioxidants.
• Modified enzymes, e.g. chymosin.
• Probiotic yogurts and drinks.
• Meat analogues, e.g. textured vegetable protein (TVP), mycoprotein and tofu.
• Functional foods, e.g. cholesterol-lowering spread.

The noodles are pre-gelatinised, so boiled water will re-heat and 'cook' them

Modified starch may be used to prevent syneresis or act as a fat replacer in low-fat meals

Key terms

Enhancers – substances that improve or add a desirable quality.

Syneresis – the process by which a liquid separates from a gel.

Activity

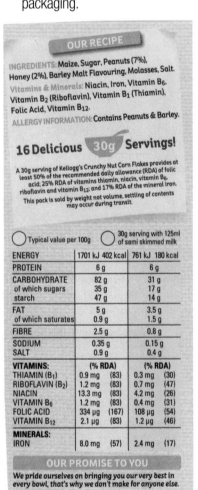

Collect examples of food products where modified starch appears on the ingredients list on the packaging.

OUR RECIPE

INGREDIENTS: Maize, Sugar, Peanuts (7%), Honey (2%), Barley Malt Flavouring, Molasses, Salt.
Vitamins & Minerals: Niacin, Iron, Vitamin B6, Vitamin B2 (Riboflavin), Vitamin B1 (Thiamin), Folic Acid, Vitamin B12.
ALLERGY INFORMATION: Contains Peanuts & Barley.

16 Delicious 30g Servings!

A 30g serving of Kellogg's Crunchy Nut Corn Flakes provides at least 50% of the recommended daily allowance (RDA) of folic acid; 25% RDA of vitamins thiamin, niacin, vitamin B6, riboflavin and vitamin B12; and 17% RDA of the mineral iron.
This pack is sold by weight not volume, settling of contents may occur during transit.

	Typical value per 100g	30g serving with 125ml of semi skimmed milk
ENERGY	1701 kJ 402 kcal	761 kJ 180 kcal
PROTEIN	6 g	6 g
CARBOHYDRATE	82 g	31 g
of which sugars	35 g	17 g
starch	47 g	14 g
FAT	5 g	3.5 g
of which saturates	0.9 g	1.5 g
FIBRE	2.5 g	0.8 g
SODIUM	0.35 g	0.15 g
SALT	0.9 g	0.4 g
VITAMINS:	**(% RDA)**	**(% RDA)**
THIAMIN (B1)	0.9 mg (83)	0.3 mg (30)
RIBOFLAVIN (B2)	1.2 mg (83)	0.7 mg (47)
NIACIN	13.3 mg (83)	4.2 mg (26)
VITAMIN B6	1.2 mg (83)	0.4 mg (31)
FOLIC ACID	334 µg (167)	108 µg (54)
VITAMIN B12	2.1 µg (83)	1.2 µg (46)
MINERALS:		
IRON	8.0 mg (57)	2.4 mg (17)

OUR PROMISE TO YOU

We pride ourselves on bringing you our very best in every bowl, that's why we don't make for anyone else.
If you have any comments or queries we would love to hear from you:

BY PHONE: UK: 0800 626066
ROI: 1800 626066

Examples of where modified starch is used in foods products:

- Hot drinks and savoury sauces
- Pot snacks
- Cook-chill meals
- French dressing

In French dressing, the hydrophobic part of the starch wraps around the oil droplet, so the hydrophilic (water loving) part of the starch is in contact with the vinegar. This keeps the oil droplets suspended in the vinegar.

Stretch and challenge

Read the following statement:

Today sees the launch of 'Zero waste events: a 2020 vision', a new initiative with the goal of no waste being sent to landfill from UK events by the end of the decade.

WRAP (2nd April 2013)

- Find out what local councils are doing to promote zero waste.
- Write an article for your school magazine promoting zero waste.

Check your understanding

What is meant by modified starch? Give one advantage of its use in a food product.

Exam practice

1. Over 25% of household rubbish is made up of food packaging material and there is growing concern over this issue. Discuss ways of reducing household packaging and rubbish by:

   a) The retailer. [3]

   b) The consumer. [3]

2. Appropriate packaging and clear labelling of food is essential to the consumer. Discuss this in relation to:

   a) Types of packaging. [6]

   b) Food labelling. [6]

Topic 10: Cooking food

What will I learn?

- **Why some foods need to be cooked.**
- **How food is cooked.**
- **How heat travels.**

10.1 How and why food is cooked

Foods are cooked for different reasons:

- To make the food easier to chew, swallow and digest.
- To destroy harmful bacteria and poisons and so make some foods safe to eat.
- To make foods more attractive and appealing. To develop flavour (taste).
- To provide hot food when the weather is cold.
- To allow some food products to rise, thicken and set to get the result required.

10.2 Heat transfer

> ### Key terms
>
> **Conduction** – when heat passes from molecule to molecule in solids or liquids.
>
> **Convection** – when heat travels around in a circular movement through air or liquids.
>
> **Radiation** – when heat travels directly in waves or rays.

Heat is a type of energy. Heat energy is passed from one material to food by three different methods called **conduction, convection** and **radiation**.

Conduction

Conduction is when heat passes through a solid material such as metal pans and food itself. Heat is conducted from molecule to molecule in solids or liquid. Metals used for tins, baking tins and pans are good conductors, which means that heat transfer is easy. Water is also a good conductor. Other materials such as wood and plastic are poor conductors; heat does not pass easily through these materials.

heat source

Conduction

Convection

Heat travels through air and liquid. Heat rises and falls, as it cools down it sets up circular movements called convection currents. Ovens are heated by convection currents. Convection currents also happen when a liquid is heated in a saucepan.

heat source

Convection

Radiation

Radiated heat travels in waves or rays through space from the source of heat to the food. The direct heat hits the food, the heat is absorbed and the food cooks. There are different types of waves or rays such as infrared and microwaves.

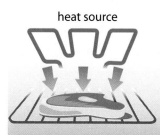

heat source

Radiation

Activities

1. Match the following food examples to the reasons for cooking: chicken, loaf of bread, tomato soup, cheese sauce, potatoes, curry, a quiche.

Reasons for cooking	Example
To make the food easier to chew, swallow and digest	
To destroy harmful bacteria and make the food safe to eat	
To provide hot food when the weather is cold	
To allow some food products to rise	
To allow some food products to thicken	
To allow some food products to set	
To develop flavour	

2. Match the description to method of heat transfer

    - Heat is transferred from the hob to the pan   radiation
    - Heat is transferred from the gas flame to the food   convection
    - Heat is transferred through the liquid to the food   conduction

Check your understanding

1. Name three methods of heat transfer.

2. Name the method of heat transfer for each of the following:
    a) Boiling a potato.
    b) Toasting bread.
    c) Baking biscuits.

3. Explain why a wooden spoon is used when stirring a hot mixture in a saucepan on the hob.

hob

oven

grill (in the top of the oven) which can also be above the hob or in a separate unit

10.3 Cookers and microwave ovens

Features of a cooker

In a fan-assisted oven, a fan moves the hot air around and, as a result, the food cooks more quickly. The heat is evenly spread around the oven so food cooks for the same amount of time on each oven shelf.

In other non-fan-assisted ovens, the food cooks at different temperatures depending on where the shelf is; the food on top cooks the fastest. A **thermostat** controls the heat chosen for cooking. A **timer** controls the cooking at pre-set times for automatic cooking.

Microwave cookers

Microwaves cook the food by radiation. The microwaves are given off by a magnetron inside the oven. The microwaves are absorbed by the food and make the molecules vibrate very fast so that they produce heat to cook the food. The microwaves penetrate the food to 3–5 cm.

Microwaves do not cook food evenly. There can be **cold spots** in the food. Inside the microwave there is a turntable which allows the microwaves to hit the food. Some food needs stirring occasionally.

Some foods such as bread, cakes and pastry dishes do not cook successfully in a microwave oven because the oven does not brown or produce a crisp crust. Combination microwave ovens allow you to switch from ordinary microwave cooking to conventional cooking which browns the food.

Microwave ovens take up very little space and use less electricity than a conventional cooker. They are very useful for thawing, reheating and cooking food quickly. The food can be served in the cooking dish, which saves time.

Microwaves can pass through material such as glass, plastic, china but not metal. Metal containers are not suitable for using in an ordinary microwave oven.

Many ready meals and processed foods are available which can be cooked from frozen in a microwave oven. Food packaging has cooking symbols which tell us the time and the temperature needed to cook products and whether you can use a cooker, a microwave or both.

> ### Key terms
>
> **Microwaves** – waves that vibrate the fat and water, producing heat.
>
> **Cold spots** – parts in the food where the heat has not penetrated.

A microwave cooker uses less electricity

10.4 Cooking methods

Method	Details and suitable foods	Advantages	Disadvantages
Boiling	Cooking food in water Vegetables, ham eggs	Fairly quick and healthy method	Loss of water-soluble vitamins. Vegetables lose their crispness
Steaming	Cooking food above boiling water Vegetables, fish	Colour and texture of food kept, no loss of water-soluble vitamins	May steam up the kitchen
Stewing or braising	Cooking food in a liquid	Good for tenderising meat, good flavour and nutritive value	Slow
Microwaving	Cooking by microwaves Most foods are suitable	Quick, uses little fuel, less vitamin loss	Food can easily overcook. Food may not look attractive
Pressure cooking	Cooking food in liquid above boiling point	Quick, saves loss of water-soluble vitamins	Food may not be as tasty
Stir-frying	Frying in very little oil Vegetables, shellfish, strips of meat	Crunchy texture, healthy method	Needs constant stirring
Frying	Cooking food in fat or oil Eggs, bacon, fish, sausages	Food is crisp and tasty	Adds fat to the food, food needs to watched
Grilling	Cooking food fierce heat or red glow Steak, chicken breast, bacon, sausages, burgers	Healthy method, quick	Food needs to be watched, can easily burn
Baking	Cooking food in the oven Bread, cakes, scones, biscuits, puddings	Adds flavour, good appearance	Takes a long time
Roasting	Cooking food in the oven with fat or oil Meat, vegetables	Good appearance and flavour, crisp outside	Takes a long time, extra fat added

A contact grill which cooks both sides of the food at the same time

Deep frying using an electric deep fryer which has a thermostat to control the temperature

Shallow frying

Stir-frying using a wok

Grilling

- Foods should be up to 3.5 cm thick.
- Food should be of even thickness.
- Meat should be cuts which will tenderise easily, for example chops, steaks.
- The fat melts and drains away into the pan.
- Foods need to be turned during cooking.
- Contact grills cook food both sides and the fat drains into a special drip tray.

Frying

- Uses hot oil or fat.
- Food can either be **shallow fried** or **deep fried**.
- Food soaks up some oil or fat during cooking.
- Some foods such as fish are coated in breadcrumbs or batter before frying.
- The oil or fat needs to be at the correct temperature before placing food in the pan.
- The temperature needs to be carefully controlled otherwise food will burn. Most foods are fried at a temperature of around 180°C. Use a thermometer to check the temperature of the oil or fat.
- Frying food needs extra care and attention because the oil or fat can catch fire if overheated.
- Keep the frying oil clean by straining after use to remove bits of food. Change oil used for frying often.

Stir-frying

- Can be carried out in a wok or large deep frying pan.
- Popular method for Chinese cooking.
- Food used is finely chopped, shredded or sliced.
- The food is tossed around the pan quickly until cooked.
- Food should be crunchy and crisp, not over cooked.

Barbecuing

- Food is cooked over metal grills over hot, glowing charcoal.
- Food needs to be turned frequently.
- Food should be cooked right through, not just on the outside.
- Suitable foods include chicken pieces or joints, steaks, sausages, burgers, mackerel, herring, corn on the cob, mushrooms and tomatoes.
- Food needs to be brushed with oil or soaked in a **marinade** before cooking

Stewing

- A gentle slow method where the flavour of the food develops during the cooking.
- Suitable for tenderising tougher cuts of meat such as stewing steak and shin of beef.

- The food is usually placed in the pan with liquid such as stock, and other foods such as vegetables.
- Method is used for cooking fruit and pulse vegetables.
- Can be carried out on the hob, in the oven or using a slow cooker.

A slow cooker, saves on fuel, is controlled by a thermostat and can be left on while you are out

A pressure cooker cooks food quickly

Poached egg on toast, a popular breakfast dish

Poaching

Poaching is cooking food very gently in a small amount of water. Only a few bubbles should appear in the cooking water, which is heated to just below **simmering** point. Examples of foods which are poached are eggs and fish.

Steaming

- Food is cooked in the steam coming from the boiling water in the bottom pan.
- Food cooked by steaming is easy to digest and very healthy.
- Few vitamins and minerals are lost because the food does not touch the water.
- There are several methods: placing a plate over a pan of water, using a special steamer pan or a plastic steamer in the microwave.

A tiered steamer where several foods can be cooked at the same time

Activities

1. Explain why using a contact grill is a healthy method of cooking. List suitable foods for cooking using this method.

2. Carry out a task comparing cooking burgers using a traditional grill and a contact grill.

   Comment on any difference in appearance, flavour, shrinkage and fat loss.

Check your understanding

1. Explain how heat is transferred to the food when boiling potatoes.

2. Describe how a microwave oven cooks food.

Key terms

Shallow frying – cooking food in a small amount of fat.

Deep frying – cooking food in a large deep pan with oil several centimetres deep.

Marinade – soaking meat in an acid such as lemon juice, vinegar or alcohol which changes the protein structure, tenderising the meat.

Simmering – a low heat boil with only a few bubbles appearing on the surface of the liquid.

10.5 Effects of heat on food

Changes take place during the cooking of food which can affect the appearance, flavour, texture and nutritive value of the food. All the nutrients are affected by heat in some way as described below.

Key terms

Gelatinisation – when starch breaks down when heated with a liquid to thicken a mixture.

Caramelisation – when sugar is heated to become a golden brown colour.

Denaturation – when a protein changes its structure.

Coagulation – when egg protein becomes solid on heating.

Starch

- Starch turns to dextrin in dry heat. A crust forms on bread and cakes. The dextrin makes the loaf crispy and turns toast brown. If the food burns, the carbohydrate is lost.
- In liquid, the starch granules swell, absorb liquid and **gelatinise**. This enables soups and sauces to thicken.

Sugar

- Sugar dissolves, changes colour and **caramelises** to a brown colour. This is used when making crème brulée, when the sugar topping is browned under the grill or using a blowtorch.

Fats

- Solid fat turns to liquid.
- Smoke is given off at a high temperature and the fat burns.
- Different fats and oils have different melting temperatures. (See Topic 11.3 Basic ingredients on page 113.)

Protein

- Protein **denatures** and changes, it then **coagulates** and sets.
- Some proteins such as meat harden; some proteins such as egg turn from liquid to solid.

Dietary fibre

- Fibre softens when heated with liquid.

Vitamins

- Fat-soluble vitamins A and D are not affected by heat.
- Water-soluble vitamins B and C dissolve in liquid.
- High temperature cooking methods such as frying destroy the vitamins.
- Vitamin C is easily lost when preparing and cooking green vegetables.

Minerals

- There is very little loss during cooking.

Check your understanding

1. What is caramelisation?

2. What happens to the following during cooking:

   a) Dietary fibre?

   b) Vitamin C?

3. Explain the meaning of the following. Give an example of each.

   a) Caramelisation

   b) Coagulation

   c) Gelatinisation

4. What happens when vitamins and minerals are heated?

Activity

Describe the changes that take place when the following are cooked:
a) A cheese sauce.
b) Scrambled eggs.
c) Toast.

Stretch and challenge

Barbecuing is a popular method of cooking food.

a) State the method of heat transfer when cooking food on a barbecue.

b) Explain how you would make sure that the food was cooked safely.

c) Suggest suitable foods for serving at a summer barbecue.

Exam practice

1. Name the method of heat transfer and explain how to ensure a quality result when cooking the following:

   a) A grilled lamb chop. [3]

   b) A baked potato. [3]

2. Different methods of cooking affect foods in a variety of ways. Discuss the benefits of:

   a) Slow cooking tougher cuts of meat. [2]

   b) Steaming fresh green vegetables. [4]

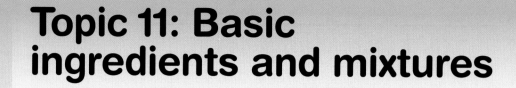

Topic 11: Basic ingredients and mixtures

What will I learn?
- Basic ingredients used in cooking.
- How the ingredients behave during cooking.

11.1 Properties and functions of ingredients

The properties of an ingredient mean its qualities and characteristics, for example:

- Whether it is liquid or solid.
- How it reacts to other ingredients.
- How it changes during cooking.

The functions of an ingredient mean, for example:

- What job it performs.
- The reason why it is used.

Properties and functions	Description	Example
Adding colour	People are attracted to colourful food	Garnish, e.g. tomato slice Decoration, e.g. cherry on a cake
Adding flavour	The taste of food is important and we like a variety – sweet, salty, spicy, strong-flavoured foods	Herbs, pepper, spices and strong-flavoured foods such as cheese, chocolate and bacon
Adding texture	Different textures in food add 'mouth feel'	Crunchy topping on ice cream, nuts in a salad
Aerating	Making food lighter by introducing air, a gas or steam to a mixture	Raising agents such as baking powder, whisking eggs, yeast in bread
Binding	Making dry ingredients stick together with an ingredient	Egg to bind fish cakes, water to bind flour and fat in pastry making
Bulking	Adding an ingredient such as a starchy food to stretch the volume of the mixture	Adding breadcrumbs to a burger mixture
Emulsifying	Bringing two liquids together	Egg yolk in mayonnaise
Glazing	Brushing egg on top of baked goods to give a brown appearance and shine	Pastries and scones
Preserving	To lengthen the shelf life of a food, or keep food longer	Sugar in jam making, vinegar in chutneys
Setting	To turn in solid or semi-solid	Gelatine in jellies, egg in a quiche
Shortening	To make crisp and crumbly	Fat in pastry making and some types of cakes
Sweetening	To make sweet	Sugar, honey, syrup and ingredients such as dried fruit
Thickening	Using flours, starchy vegetables to make a mixture thicker	Flour in sauces, potato in soups

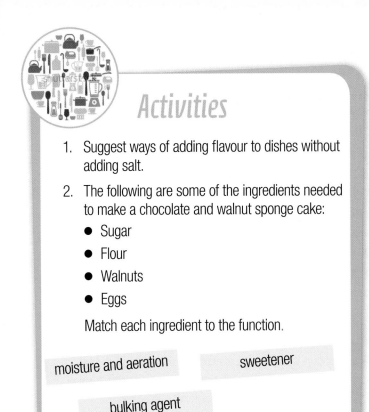

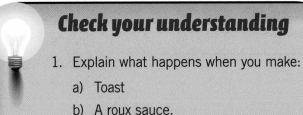

Activities

1. Suggest ways of adding flavour to dishes without adding salt.

2. The following are some of the ingredients needed to make a chocolate and walnut sponge cake:
   - Sugar
   - Flour
   - Walnuts
   - Eggs

   Match each ingredient to the function.

   moisture and aeration   sweetener

   bulking agent

   texture

Check your understanding

1. Explain what happens when you make:
   a) Toast
   b) A roux sauce.

2. Give two examples of ingredients that have the following properties in cooking:
   a) Thickening
   b) Shortening
   c) Setting.

   Name an example of a dish in each case.

11.2 Acids and alkalis

Acids and alkalis affect food during preparation and cooking. Acids and alkalis are measured on scale called a **pH scale**.

Key term

pH scale – the scale for measuring acids and alkalis.

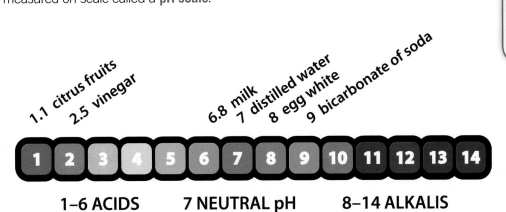

1.1 citrus fruits
2.5 vinegar
6.8 milk
7 distilled water
8 egg white
9 bicarbonate of soda

| 1 | 2 | 3 | 4 | 5 | 6 | 7 | 8 | 9 | 10 | 11 | 12 | 13 | 14 |

1–6 ACIDS   **7 NEUTRAL pH**   **8–14 ALKALIS**

Effect of acids

1. Acids such as lemon juice stop enzymic browning in fruits such as apples, pears and bananas. Once cut, the enzymes in the fruit react with the oxygen in the air and the fruit begins to turn brown. The citric acid in citrus fruits stops this from happening.

2. Acids can curdle a sauce which has been thickened with a starchy food such as flour. **Curdling** is when a sauce separates and the **consistency** is changed.

3. Acids can tenderise meat when it is left to soak in a marinade. Lemon juice, wine vinegar and yogurt are examples of ingredients used in a marinade. The acid helps to break down the meat protein and make it more tender when cooked.

4. Adding a small amount of acid such as cream of tartar, lemon juice or vinegar when whisking egg white helps to make them foamy. The acid stabilises the egg white and enables them to whisk more successfully.

5. Some types of fish are marinated in citrus fruit, which breaks down the protein and 'cooks' it. This process is used in making a South American dish called Ceviche. The fish is eaten in this state.

6. Adding vinegar to vegetables such as pickling onions stops growth of bacteria. Bacteria will not grow and multiply in acidic conditions.

Effect of alkali

The most common type of alkali used in cooking is bicarbonate of soda. It is used in some cake recipes with an acidic ingredient such as buttermilk to make them rise. Alkalis destroy vitamin C and should not be used when cooking green vegetables.

11.3 Basic ingredients

Flour

(See also Topic 3.8 Cereals on page 76.)

Flour is made from cereals and plants. Examples are: wheat flour from wheat, potato flour from potatoes, cornflour from maize, barley flour from barley and rice flour from rice. Flours contain the carbohydrate starch.

Wheat flour contains gluten. Gluten is a mixture of two proteins called gliadin and glutenin found in most cereals. The amount of gluten varies with the type of cereal and type of flour. Gluten, when mixed with liquid, forms long strands and becomes stretchy and elastic. When flour mixtures are heated, the mixture is pushed up and the gluten sets, forming a framework or crust.

People who have coeliac disease must avoid foods containing gluten.

Functions and properties of flour

Flours are starchy ingredients. When flour and liquid are mixed together and heated, the starch granules absorb the liquid. As the liquid gets hotter the granules swell to make a paste called a gel. The granules burst and the mixture thickens completely. The starchy taste disappears and the mixture should look shiny and smooth. This process is called **gelatinisation.** Gelatinisation happens during the making of any sauce, gravy and custard where a type of flour is used to thicken. If the sauce is left to cool and harden or is frozen, the gel leaks and water is forced out of the structure. This is called **retrogradation.**

Starch is changed to dextrin when cooked in dry heat such as baking or grilling. This gives baked products such as cakes and biscuits a brown colour and crisp texture.

Different types of flours

Different types of wheat flour

Flour is classified according to:

- How much and which parts of the grain are used.
- The type of wheat used.

Name	Description	Uses
Strong plain, white or wholemeal	Contains more than 10% protein, high in gluten.	Bread mixtures, choux pastry and batters
Soft plain, white or wholemeal	Contain less than 10% protein, 72% grain, low % gluten	Short crust pastry, cakes and biscuits
Self-raising, white or wholemeal	A soft flour, less than 10% protein, baking powder added	Cakes and scones
Durum wheat	More than 10% protein, gluten is very tough, does not stretch easily	Fresh pasta

- Wholemeal flour is 80–90% grain.
- Wheatgerm flour is 90% grain.
- Stoneground flour is 100% grain.
- Granary flour is a mixture of rye flour and wheat flour with whole grain and malt extract added.

Sugars

Sugar is obtained from sugar beet and sugar cane. It is extracted as a black syrup which contains natural impurities called molasses. Brown sugars keep some of this natural syrup and have a special flavour of their own.

Sugars dissolve in any liquid. When heated, sugar crystals melt, form a syrup and then caramelise (turn a brown colour). Further heating burns the sugar giving off smoke and a smell.

Functions and properties of sugar

- To add sweetness

  Used in many recipes and added to fruit, sauces and ready-made foods to make them more acceptable to eat.

- To add texture

  Sugar softens the gluten in baked items when they are cooked. This adds a soft crumb with a moist texture.

- To trap air

  Fat and sugar are creamed together, eggs and sugar are whisked together to make cakes and whisked sponges. When whisked with egg white, sugar makes the foam stable.

- To add colour

  The sugar **caramelises** when heated and browns foods such as cakes and biscuits during baking.

- To preserve

  Sugar is a main ingredient in jam and marmalade making. It helps the product keep for a long time.

- To help **fermentation**

  Sugar helps to speed up the action of yeast to produce carbon dioxide in bread making.

Key terms

Caramelisation – the browning of sugar when heated.

Fermentation – the breakdown of carbohydrates in bread and beer making.

Stabiliser – a substance that allows fat and water to mix.

Different types of sugar

Different types of sugar

- Granulated
- Caster sugar
- Icing sugar
- Brown sugar as demerara, soft brown, dark brown, muscavado. All have a stronger flavour than white and are used for making cakes and biscuits.

Sugar substitutes are available. These can be used in recipes instead of sugar to lower the amount of kcalories. Two examples are:

- Splenda sugar made from molasses, sweetener, humectant and **stabiliser**.
- Fruisana made from fructose. Fructose is sweeter than ordinary sugar so you use less.

Examples of a sugar substitute

Fats and oils

Fats are generally used for spreading on bread and in cooking to fry and roast. Oils are used in salad dressings for frying and roasting. We are recommended to cut down on the amount of fats we eat, particularly saturated fats which are high in cholesterol and are linked to heart disease.

Functions and properties of fats

- To shorten

  Fats make pastry products and cakes soft and crumbly. When used in cake and pastry recipes, the fat coats the flour particles with a waterproof layer, which stops the gluten in the flour from forming long strands. This gives a 'melt in the mouth' texture because the fat has shortened the gluten strands.

- To aerate

  When fat and sugar are creamed the fat will trap tiny air bubbles.

- To add flavour and moisture

  Fat stops water from evaporating and gives food a longer 'shelf life'.

- To fry

  Fats and oils are suitable for frying to give flavour and add a crisp texture. Vegetable oils have a high smoke point and are good for frying as the high temperature seals the food on the outside, locking in the flavour.

Name of fat or oil	Smoke point
Lard	205°C
Most vegetable oils	232°C
Vegetable shortenings	188°C

Different types of fats and oils:

Types of fat

- Butter

  Made from milk, it has a good flavour, and is high in saturated fat. It is available as salted, slightly salted and unsalted. Used for spreading, baking, shallow frying. Ghee is clarified unsalted butter used in Asian cooking.

- Lard

  Made from the fat surrounding the internal organs of a pig. It is high in saturated fat and is used to make pastry and for frying.

- Margarine

  Made from a range of animal and vegetable fats. Can be hardened by hydrogenation. Used for spreading and for baking because it mixes easily with other ingredients.

- Oil

  Made from seeds and nuts. They include corn, rapeseed, walnut, soya and olive. Used for making dressings, for frying, baking and roasting.

- Reduced fat spreads

  Contain 40–80% fat, which is up to half the amount compared with butter and margarine which are 80% fat. They are useful in low fat diets and weight reducing diets. Used for spreading mostly. They contain a large amount of water and as a result are not suitable for cooking.

- Solid vegetable fat

  Made purely from vegetables. Contains less saturated fat than lard and is used in pastry making and frying.

- Suet

  Made from the fat surrounding the kidneys of an animal. Used to make dumplings and suet pastry. 'Vegetarian' suet is available for cooking.

Activities

1. Explain the function of sugar in the following recipes:
   a) Blackberry jam
   b) Rock cakes
   c) Meringues
   d) Crème caramel.

2. Name two fats that are suitable for the following:
   a) Pastry making
   b) Cake making.
   Give reasons for your choices.

Check your understanding

1. Suggest one type of fat or oil suitable for frying. Give a reason for your choice.

2. Name three different types of flours. Suggest when and why they are used.

3. Give two examples of ingredients that perform each of the following functions:
   a) Aerating
   b) Binding dry ingredients
   c) Shortening.

11.4 Raising agents

Raising agents are used to make mixtures light. They work by producing bubbles of gas which expand when heated, pushing up the mixture. Some gas escapes and some is trapped in the mixture as it cooks and sets. The raising agents are:

- Carbon dioxide
- Air
- Steam.

Carbon dioxide

This is produced in two ways:

- Chemical raising agents – baking powder and bicarbonate of soda. Once these powders are mixed with a liquid and heated they produce carbon dioxide gas. Self-raising flour is ready mixed with baking powder.
- Yeast – a single-cell plant which needs moisture, food and warmth to ferment and produces carbon dioxide.

Yeast is used as a raising agent in bread making.

Air

Air is introduced into mixtures by:

- Sieving flour
- Creaming fat and sugar
- Whisking eggs and sugar
- Beating eggs for batters
- Whisking egg whites for meringues
- Rubbing fat into flour
- Rolling and folding pastry.

Fresh yeast is a living plant   *Dried yeast or quick acting yeast*

Steam

When water is heated it evaporates as steam. Steam is used as a raising agent in mixtures which are very watery, for example batters and choux pastry.

Examples of mechanical methods of introducing air into mixtures (above)

Pancakes made with batter

Chocolate éclairs made with choux pastry

Key term

Raising agent – used to make mixtures light.

Activity

Use a recipe for making cupcakes. Read the method and list the raising agents used to make the cupcakes rise.

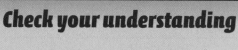

Check your understanding

1. Name three raising agents.
2. Describe ways in which air is introduced into mixtures.
3. Name the raising agent in the following:
   a) Bread
   b) A whisked mixture sponge
   c) Yorkshire pudding.

11.5 Basic mixtures

Bread

Bread is a staple food in the UK and other countries. It is a good source of carbohydrate, protein, B vitamins, dietary fibre and calcium and iron. There are many different types of bread from all over the world on sale.

Most of the bread we eat is white, brown or wholemeal, made from wheat flour.

- White bread is made from white flour, which is fortified with added vitamins, iron and calcium.
- Brown bread is made from flour with some bran and wheat germ removed.
- Wholemeal bread is made from wholemeal flour. It contains more fibre than white bread.

Other popular breads include granary, malted, rye, spelt, multi grain, chia and soda bread.

Bread is made from strong flour, yeast, liquid and sometimes fat:

- The ingredients are combined to make a sticky dough. The dough is kneaded to develop the gluten and to make it smooth.
- The dough is left to rise or **prove** in a warm place.
- When cooked in the oven, the yeast produces carbon dioxide, gas bubbles and alcohol.
- The gas bubbles expand and push up the dough.
- The gluten in the dough stretches with **kneading** and cooking.
- Water is turned into steam and this helps to make the dough rise.
- The alcohol escapes.
- At a temperature of about 75ºC, the gluten starts to set.
- The inside of the bread becomes spongy and soft and the outside forms a crust.
- The starch in the flour is changed to dextrin, which caramelises to give bread its colour.
- The bread is cooked when it sounds hollow when tapped underneath.

A wide variety of popular breads are available

Key terms

Proving – allowing time for the dough to rise.

Kneading – mixing and stretching the dough by hand or mechanically.

Activity

Match the name of the bread to the correct picture.

Find out which country they all come from and what cereal they are made from.

| chapatti | soda | crumpet | bara brith |

| brioche | baguette | griddle scone | naan |

| focaccia | croissant | challah | ciabatta |

Check your understanding

1. Name the process shown in the picture.

2. Name the raising agent used to make bread rise.

3. Explain what happens during the baking of bread.

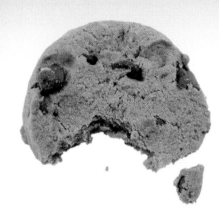

Biscuits

- When the biscuit dough is put in the oven, the fat melts and is absorbed by the starch in the flour.
- Any air trapped in the dough expands and the biscuits rise very slightly.
- The starch and gluten both set and the biscuit becomes crisp with a 'melt in the mouth' texture.
- Biscuits should have a pale golden brown colour.

Cakes

Cakes are made using the following methods:

- Rubbed in
- Creaming
- Whisking
- Melting.

These changes take place during cooking:

- The air trapped in the mixture expands and makes the mixture rise.
- The eggs help the mixture to set and add colour.
- The sugar melts and softens the gluten to make the cake soft.
- The fat melts and is absorbed by the starch in the flour.
- If there is raising agent in the mixture, it gives off CO_2 gas which expands with the heat and makes the cake rise.
- A golden crust is formed on the outside.

Pastry

The following are types of pastry:

- Short crust
- Flaky and puff
- Choux pastry.

The following changes take place during cooking.

Short crust:

- The fat melts and is absorbed by the starch in the flour.
- Any air trapped in the dough expands and makes the dough rise but because the gluten strands are short, the dough cannot stretch very much.
- The starch and the gluten set and the pastry becomes crisp.
- The heat gives the cooked pastry a golden brown colour.

Flaky and puff pastry:

- The fat melts and is absorbed by the starch in the flour.
- The air trapped between the layers of dough expands and pushes up the dough.
- The water in the dough turns to steam which also pushes up the dough.
- The gluten and the starch set and the pastry becomes crisp and flaky.

Choux pastry:

- The melted fat and the water are heated in the pan, and are absorbed by the starch in the flour.
- When the pastry is put in the oven, the water turns to steam, which makes the pastry rise quickly.
- The gluten and the starch start to set and the pastry turns a brown colour.
- The choux pastry does not set until the last minutes of cooking. It is important not to open the oven door during at this time, otherwise the choux pastry will collapse.

Batters

A batter is a mixture of flour, eggs, liquid such as milk. There are three main types. All are made in the same way using the same main ingredients. The quantity of liquid varies and this affects the **consistency.** The types are:

- Pouring – a thin batter used to make pancakes, Yorkshire pudding and toad-in-the-hole.
- Coating – a thicker batter used to make fritters or to coat pieces of raw fish before frying.
- A tempura is a light Japanese batter made from plain flour, cornflour, sea salt and sparkling water which is used for coating vegetables before frying in hot oil.

Sauces

Sauces are added to food for the following reasons:

- To add flavour
- To add colour
- To moisten food
- To bind ingredients together
- To add nutrients
- To add variety and interest to dishes.

The main types of sauces are:

- A basic white sauce, called a **roux** sauce

    A roux is made by melting the fat and adding the flour until a paste is made. The starch in the flour absorbs the fat. Milk is added, the sauce is heated and the starch granules swell and cause the sauce to thicken. The sauce then gelatinises (becomes jelly-like).

    A white sauce can be made using the one-stage method where all ingredients are placed in a pan and heated until thickened.

- A cornflour sauce

    Milk and cornflour are mixed together and heated until the starch granules absorb the liquid and begin to swell. This causes the sauce to thicken and gelatinise. There is no fat in a cornflour sauce.

Other types of sauce include tomato and pesto. A coulis is a fruit-based sauce using soft fruits such as strawberries, raspberries, blackcurrants, blueberries.

Key terms

Consistency – the thickness or thinness of a food mixture.

Roux – a mixture of flour and fat that is cooked briefly and used as the thickening base of a sauce or soup.

Activities

1. List sweet and savoury dishes where a sauce forms part of the dish, e.g. cauliflower cheese.

2. You have made a Victoria sponge which is well risen, light, spongy and golden brown.

   a) Name two ingredients that will have helped the Victoria sponge to rise.

   b) Name two ingredients that will have added colour and flavour.

   c) What other factors will have contributed to the success in making your Victoria sponge?

Check your understanding

1. Name the methods of cake making. Give an example for each method.

2. Name the types of pastry. Give an example of a dish made from each type of pastry.

3. a) What is the meaning of a 'roux' sauce?

   b) Give reasons why sauces are added to foods.

4. Describe what happens to the following ingredients when a batter is baked in the oven:
   - The liquid
   - The egg
   - The starch in the flour.

Stretch and challenge

Explain what has gone wrong with each of the following mixtures:

a) A Swiss roll which is flat and crispy and cracks when it is rolled up.

b) Bread rolls which are heavy and chewy.

c) A white sauce which is lumpy and too thick.

d) Chocolate éclairs which are flat and heavy.

Exam practice

1. Suggest why herbs and spices are used in dishes instead of salt. [4]

2. Explain how to achieve a quality result when making and cooking short crust pastry. [6]

Topic 12: Equipment

What will I learn?

- **Different equipment used to store, prepare and cook food.**
- **Choice and use of the equipment.**

There is a variety of equipment, both small and large, available to help save time and energy when preparing and cooking food. Large equipment includes:

- Food processors
- Bread machines
- Slow cookers
- Contact grills
- Blenders and whisks
- Electric steamers
- Pasta machines
- Rice cookers
- Juicers
- Waffle makers.

All food preparation and cooking equipment may or may not be useful. The following points need to be considered before buying:

- Cost.
- The amount of use it will have / is it really useful?
- Ease of cleaning.
- The amount of storage space available in the kitchen.

12.1 Refrigerators and freezers

Refrigerators and freezers keep food safe for longer. Refrigerators keep food cool and fresher for short periods of time. Freezers freeze food to keep it fresh for long-term storage.

Refrigerators

The correct temperature for a refrigerator is between 1°C and 5°C.

Check the temperature with a thermometer as it is unsafe to store food if the temperature of the refrigerator is above this.

For safe food storage in the refrigerator:

- Keep food covered as this will prevent the loss of moisture from food and prevent food from drying out.

A refrigerator showing correct storage of fresh foods

A fridge freezer, with the fridge part on top and the freezer part beneath

- Raw foods should be stored below cooked foods. This will prevent cross-contamination.

- Do not overfill the refrigerator – allow a little air to move around the food.

- Regularly clean the refrigerator with clean water, no detergent.

- Check dates on food kept in the refrigerator and throw away any which are past their sell by date.

- Don't open the fridge more than necessary as this allows warm air to get in and raise the temperature inside.

- Do not put hot foods in the refrigerator as this will raise the temperature inside. Cool foods first, then refrigerate.

Freezers

The correct temperature of a freezer should be –18°C or below. Check the temperature with a freezer thermometer. A freezer turns the water in foods to ice. Micro-organisms cannot grow in cold temperatures but once the food is defrosted, the micro-organisms become alive and are able to grow and multiply again.

For safe storage of frozen foods:

- Wrap food well before freezing to protect the food from **freezer burn** and from drying out. A variety of freezer bags and plastic containers are available for packaging foods for the freezer. Freezer aluminum foil and cling film are also available, which are strong and prevent smells transferring from one food to another.

- Defrost and clean the freezer twice a year.

- Keep the freezer as full as possible. An empty or half-full freezer uses more electricity to keep temperature at –18°C.

- Do not refreeze food once defrosted.

Star ratings are found on frozen food compartments and on frozen food packaging. These give storage instructions and the 'shelf life' of commercial frozen foods in a home freezer.

An upright freezer

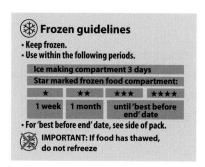

Star markings on a freezer and the snowflake logo

Shopping for frozen foods

Frozen foods should arrive home in their frozen state if they are to be stored in the home freezer. Cool bags and boxes are ideal for carrying frozen foods home. They are insulated to stop the food from becoming warm and defrosting.

Pack all frozen foods together tightly using ice packs if using ordinary shopping bags. Place frozen food in the boot of the car for transporting home, as it is cooler than inside the car. Unpack foods straight after arriving home and place in the freezer.

A cool bag

Key term

Freezer burn – caused by water molecules leaving the food. It appears as greyish-brown, dried out patches on the surfaces of frozen or thawed food.

Activity

Carry out research to find out which is the most popular electrical kitchen equipment.

Explain how the equipment saves time and labour.

Check your understanding

1. List four rules for keeping food safely in:

   a) A refrigerator

   b) A freezer.

2. Discuss how labour-saving equipment can encourage people to cook at home.

Exam practice

1. Technology has helped reduce the time spent on food preparation and cooking in the home. Evaluate how technology has influenced:

   a) Equipment in the home. [5]

   b) The use of ready and partly prepared food in the home. [5]

2. Give two uses and one safety point for each of the following pieces of equipment:

   a) A food processor.

   b) A microwave oven.

   c) A deep fat fryer. [9]

Topic 13: Additives in food

What will I learn?

- Types of food that are manufactured for us.
- What goes into manufactured foods.

Colour is added to custard to make it look bright yellow

Green colouring is added to tinned peas to restore colour

Antioxidants help to prolong the shelf life of fruit juice

Food additives are substances put into processed food by food manufacturers. They may be natural, natural identical (copies of substances that occur naturally) or artificial.

The main groups are:

- Antioxidants
- Colours
- Flavour enhancers
- Sweeteners
- Emulsifiers
- Stabilisers
- Preservatives.

All additives are thoroughly tested by the government and the European Union (EU) before they are allowed to be used. The ones approved by the EU are given an 'E' number.

- **Antioxidants** decrease the chance of oils and fats in foods from combining with oxygen and changing colour or turning rancid (going off). Rancid fats smell and taste unpleasant and are a health risk. Antioxidants are also used in fruits, vegetables and juice to extend the shelf life. Vitamin C (ascorbic acid) is one of the most widely used antioxidants.

- **Colours** are used to make food look more appetising. During the processing of some food, colour can be lost so additives are used to restore the original colour, for example to restore canned marrow fat peas to their original colour. Colour additives can also be used to make the existing food colour brighter, for example adding to the yellowness of custard.

  Colour additives are either natural (e.g. curcumin (E100) is a yellow extract of turmeric roots), nature identical or artificial. Some colours are also vitamins (e.g. riboflavin and beta-carotene) and these are the only colours allowed in baby food.

- **Flavour enhancers** are used widely in savoury foods to enhance the existing flavour in the food. Monosodium glutamate is an example of a flavour enhancer.

- **Emulsifiers** help mix together ingredients like oil and water that would normally separate. **Stabilisers** prevent them from separating again. They are used for foods such as ice cream.

- **Gelling agents** are used to give foods a gel-like consistency, while thickeners increase the viscosity of foods.

- **Preservatives** are used to help keep food safe to eat for longer. Any processed food with a long shelf life is likely to include preservatives.

- **Sweeteners** are sweeter than sugar and so are only used in tiny amounts. This makes them suitable for use in products such as diet drinks which are low in kilocalories. Examples of sweeteners are sorbitol and sucralose.

- **Additives** are tested before they are used in food products but there is concern over their use. Some people are concerned that children, in particular, are consuming too many foods containing additives on a daily basis. They are concerned that the additives may have short- and long-term effects on health.

There is a concern that artificial colours and preservatives trigger hyperactive behaviour in children, and the development of particular types of cancer.

Checking the labels of food will give information on what ingredients and additives are in processed foods. People who are concerned about the use of additives should limit the amount of processed food they eat and choose natural, unprocessed foods.

Activity

Study the following label on a can of tomato soup:

Name the two main ingredients in this product.

Find out why the other ingredients have been added to the canned soup.

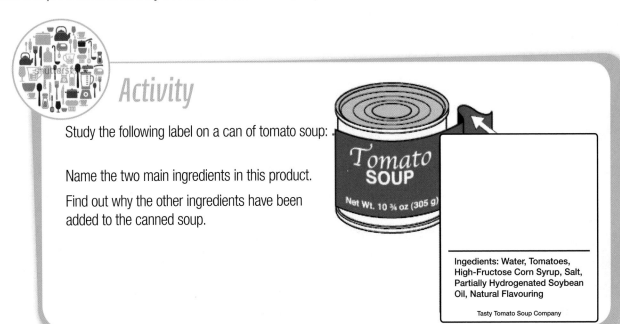

Tomato SOUP

Net Wt. 10 ¾ oz (305 g)

Ingredients: Water, Tomatoes, High-Fructose Corn Syrup, Salt, Partially Hydrogenated Soybean Oil, Natural Flavouring

Tasty Tomato Soup Company

Check your understanding

1. Name three categories of food additives.
2. Discuss the advantages and disadvantages of additives in food products.

Exam practice

Additives are widely used in food production. Evaluate the role of additives:

a) In food production.

b) To the consumer. [10]

Topic 14: Convenience foods

Convenience foods are packaged food that can be prepared quickly and easily, for example food in cans, bottles, cartons and bags. They are sold as dried, frozen and chilled products.

Some examples of convenience foods are:

- Canned – soups, baked beans, curry sauce, stews, sauces.
- Cartons – soups, sauces, drinks.
- Bottles and jars – sauces, baby food, fruit.
- Packets – dried soup, noodles, rice dishes, prepared vegetables.
- Chilled food – ready meals, wraps, filled rolls and desserts.
- Cook-chill foods – prepared and often cooked for the consumer. They are packed in containers to reheat or cook and serve at home.

Fast food is cooked, wrapped in a packet for the customer and usually eaten without the need for cutlery, e.g. burgers, fries, pizza, fish and chips, snack foods such as sandwiches, rolls, pies and pasties.

Takeaway food is food that is prepared, cooked and taken away in containers to eat at home, e.g. Indian, Chinese, Mexican meals.

Cook-chill meals have increased in popularity over the years because:

- They save time and effort.
- They make meal preparation easier.
- They have a longer shelf life.
- They are 'portion controlled'.

Who might find cook-chill meals particularly useful?

- People who have little time to prepare meals.
- People who have limited food preparation and cooking skills.
- People who have limited space and equipment in the kitchen.
- People who have certain physical disabilities and who may have difficulty in handling equipment and cooking for themselves.
- Families with fussy eaters or special diet requirements. Individual meals can be bought for them.
- Elderly people who find shopping and food preparation difficult.

Disadvantages of cook-chill meals:

- The food is not freshly prepared.
- The quality of the food may not be as good.
- They can be expensive.

- They are often high in saturated fat, salt and sugar and low in fibre.
- They often contain flavourings and preservatives to make them attractive and to make them last longer.

Check your understanding

1. Give two examples of convenience food meals.

2. Give two examples of fast foods meals.

3. Describe three advantages of convenience foods.

4. Describe two disadvantages of convenience foods.

Exam practice

The range of cook-chill ready meals available is increasing. Discuss this in relation to:

a) Reasons for their popularity. [4]

b) Value for money. [4]

Topic 15: Preservation

What will I learn?
- **What causes food to go bad.**
- **How to keep foods longer in the home.**

Bacteria, yeasts and moulds are the micro-organisms that cause food to 'go off'. The micro-organisms need food, warmth, moisture and time to multiply. Enzymes also cause food to go bad.

Preservation is a method which removes the conditions to stop the micro-organisms from multiplying. The most common methods are:

- Using high temperatures to kill the micro-organisms and stop the action of enzymes.
- Using cold temperatures to make the micro-organisms inactive and slow down chemical reaction.
- Removing water by drying the food to kill micro-organisms and prevent chemical reactions from taking place.
- Using acids to kill micro-organisms and stop the action of enzymes.
- Using sugar or salt to remove water from the micro-organisms to kill them.
- Using special packaging which removes oxygen to stop growth of micro-organisms. Examples are vacuum packing and modified atmospheric packaging. (See Topic 7 Food packaging on pages 93–94.)

There are many ways of preserving food in the home:

- Jam making
- Pickling
- Making chutney
- Freezing
- Bottling
- Drying.

Key terms

Pectin – a carbohydrate in fruit that causes jam to gel and set.

Blanching – dipping vegetables into boiling water for a few seconds and then rapidly dipping them into iced water to stop growth of enzymes.

Brine – salted water.

Jam making is a way of preserving fruit by using high heat and sugar. Fruit is stewed in water to soften it, a large amount of sugar is added and the mixture boiled to a high temperature. The combination of heat, sugar and **pectin** in the fruit causes the jam to form a gel and set when it cools down.

Pickling is a method of preserving vegetables, onions and hard-boiled eggs. An acid called acetic acid, found in vinegar, is used. The vegetables are prepared and packed into clean jars with spices, the vinegar is poured on top to cover the vegetables and the jars are sealed.

Making chutney also uses the acetic acid found in vinegar to preserve vegetables and fruits. Once prepared, the vegetables and fruits are cooked to a high temperature with vinegar, sugar, salt and spices until thick.

Freezing is a method of preserving fruits, vegetables, meat, fish and a variety of home cooked and ready meals. The temperature of the freezer should be at –18°C or below. By freezing food, the water inside turns to ice and this stops the growth of micro-organisms.

Foods for freezing must be fresh and frozen quickly to prevent large ice crystals from forming and damaging the structure of the food. Most home freezers have a 'fast freeze' control switch on them. Vegetables that are frozen should be **blanched** to stop the action of enzymes.

Once defrosted, frozen foods should be treated like fresh food as the micro-organisms will become active again once the food gets to the right temperature.

Making jam and chutney are methods of preserving fruit and vegetables in the home

Frozen food such as chicken must be thoroughly defrosted before cooking. If chicken is not thoroughly defrosted, the temperature in the centre of the chicken may not be high enough to kill the bacteria and they will multiply.

Bottling is when fruits or vegetables are prepared and placed in special glass jars, a sugar syrup or **brine** is added and the jars are sealed and heated to a very high temperature to sterilise the contents. Sterilisation will destroy the micro-organisms and the bottled fruit and vegetables will keep for several months.

Drying is a useful method of preservation for herbs and some fruits. Herbs are tied in bundles and dried upside down in a warm place where air moves around them. This removes water from the leaves and, once dried, the herbs can be stored in an airtight jar.

Activities

1. Suggest different ways of preserving the following foods:
   a) Onions
   b) Strawberries.

2. Describe how you would:
   a) Prepare a freshly made apple pie for the freezer
   b) Defrost a frozen chicken.

Check your understanding

1. Name four ways of preserving food in the home.

2. Explain how micro-organisms in food can be destroyed when:
   a) Pickling
   b) Jam making.

3. What is the correct temperature for a home freezer?

Stretch and challenge

Compare a cook-chill meal with making the same meal from scratch using fresh ingredients.

Comment on cost, nutritive value, appearance, flavour and texture.

Exam practice

1. a) Explain what is meant by 'blanching'. [2]
   b) Name two vgetables that can be blanched. [2]

2. Additives are widely used in food production. Evaluate the role of additives. [6]

Topic 16: Food spoilage

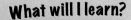

What will I learn?

- **Organisms that cause food spoilage.**

People often say that food has gone off; here we will explore what makes food go off and the differences between food spoilage caused by bacteria, yeasts and mould. To enable food to be edible for as long as possible we will also look at ways to control food spoilage.

What is food spoilage?

Food spoilage is the deterioration of food to the point where it is no longer fit to eat. Food spoilage organisms are so small that they cannot be seen without a microscope. There are three types of micro-organisms that are responsible for food spoilage: **bacteria**, **yeasts** and **mould**.

Bacteria

Bacteria are found everywhere – in soil, water, air, animals and humans. Bacteria are single-cell organisms that are so small that it takes one million to cover a pin head. Bacteria need food, warmth, moisture, time and the correct pH to grow and multiply. Some bacteria also need oxygen to grow.

Bacteria multiply rapidly in the **temperature danger zone** between 5°C and 63°C, but most are killed at temperatures of 72°C and above.

Bacteria are useful to us in food production, for example making foods such as cheese and yogurt. Some bacteria are harmful because they make toxins (poisons) which can cause food poisoning.

Some things such as salt, sugar or acid are able to destroy bacteria.

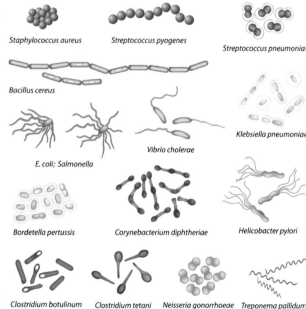

Staphylococcus aureus

Streptococcus pyogenes

Streptococcus pneumonia

Bacillus cereus

Klebsiella pneumonia

Vibrio cholerae

E. coli; Salmonella

Bordetella pertussis

Corynebacterium diphtheriae

Helicobacter pylori

Clostridium botulinum

Clostridium tetani

Neisseria gonorrhoeae

Treponema pallidum

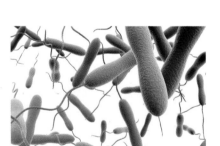

Key terms

Bacteria – single-celled organism that causes harmful food spoilage but can also be useful in food production.

Yeast – one-celled fungi that ferments.

Mould – a type of fungi.

Temperature danger zone – 5–63°C, the temperature in which bacteria grow most rapidly.

Yeasts

Yeasts are microscopic, one-celled fungi. They are found in soil, in the air and on the surface of plants.

Although yeasts can cause food spoilage in foods such as jam, they can also be useful in food production. Yeasts feed off sugars and when they mix, and warmth is

added a process called **fermentation** occurs. Fermentation creates carbon dioxide gas; this can be used in bread making to help the bread rise and to make grapes into wine, and hops into beer.

Yeasts are killed by heat, so it is important in bread making to ensure the ingredients are at the correct temperature to activate the yeast.

Mould

Moulds are a thread-like fungus. They grow in dry and acidic conditions and can tolerate a range of temperatures. They produce spores that are carried in the air. These spores settle and grow on the surface of foods such as soft fruits, bread, jam and cheese. Moulds are easy to see on food as they appear like blue, furry growth. They can be useful in food production when making blue cheese, to give them their flavour.

Most moulds, such as the mould in Stilton cheese, are harmless. Some, however, produce toxins which can be dangerous, especially to pregnant women. Moulds can be killed by heating to high temperature, e.g. when making jam.

Enzymes

Another cause of food spoilage is **enzymes**. These are not micro-organisms but chemicals that can be found in food. **Enzymatic browning** occurs in fruits such as apples, making the surface go brown when cut. Enzymes can also cause vitamin loss in food.

> ### Key terms
>
> **Fermentation** – the chemical breakdown of a substance by bacteria, yeasts or other micro-organisms.
>
> **Enzymes** – chemicals found in food that cause changes.
>
> **Enzymic browning** – the browning effect that enzymes have on fruits when exposed to the air.

Check your understanding

1. Name three types of organisms that cause food spoilage.
2. Explain how each of these organisms cause spoilage.
3. Give three examples of how micro-organisms can be useful in food production.
4. How do enzymes cause food spoilage?

Activities

1. Cut an apple, banana or aubergine in half. Leave for about 30 minutes and note what happens. Find out what you could do or add to the fruit to stop this from happening.

2. Some vegetables are blanched before they are frozen. Find out what this process means and explain why it is carried out.

16.1 Controlling food spoilage

For micro-organisms to grow, they need the following conditions:

- Food
- Moisture
- Time
- Warmth
- Neutral pH
- Air.

Growth of bacteria is slowed down if one of these conditions is removed. It is therefore important to understand how we can control the growth of micro-organisms, especially food poisoning bacteria.

Food and moisture

Some foods are more likely to cause food poisoning than others. These are called **high risk foods**. These foods are often moist foods with high protein content like chicken, meat, fish and dairy products. It is important that we store these foods correctly and eat them before their use by date or else they can go off, making them unsafe to eat.

We can extend the shelf life for high risk foods by preserving them, using methods where the moisture is no longer available for growth. Two examples of this would be:

- Freezing, where water is frozen and is no longer available to the bacteria.
- Drying, where the water has been removed.

Time

Bacteria divides in a process called **binary fission**, meaning that the number of bacteria in a product doubles approximately every 20 minutes. Providing the other conditions are correct this means that a food can go from being safe to having enough bacteria to cause illness in just a few hours.

This can be easily prevented through the correct handling of food during preparation, storage, cooking and reheating.

Follow the three simple rules below to reduce the amount of time bacteria have to multiply:

- Reduce the amount of time food is in the temperature danger zone (5–63°C).
- Try not to keep food out the refrigerator or freezer too long between buying and storing.
- Make sure that food is eaten by the 'use-by' or 'best-before' dates or it may be unsafe to eat.

Temperature control

Bacteria need warm conditions to multiply, the temperature danger zone (5–63°C) shows the temperature at which bacteria will multiply.

Examples of 'high risk foods'

	danger zone			
-18°C	5°C	37°C	63°C	100°C

Bacteria multiply most rapidly between 20 and 50°C, but their growth can be prevented by storing food below 5°C or cooking food to above 63°C.

Cool it down

When food is kept refrigerated below 5°C, the bacteria is not killed, but their growth is slowed down. When food is stored in a freezer, at –18°C bacteria stop growing, but will start multiplying again once at the correct temperature because bacteria are not killed by cold temperatures.

Heat it up

Cooking food to a high temperature is the most effective way of destroying bacteria and preventing food poisoning; however, even then, some bacteria can produce spores that survive above 63°C.

When cooking food it is important to check that it is cooked all the way through. This can be done by inserting a temperature **food probe** into the centre of the food to make sure the food it safe to eat it should reach **72°C or above** for **2 minutes.**

When food is not being eaten straight away there is a renewed risk of bacteria being transferred to the food and given the correct conditions it will start to multiply again.

- Where food is being kept hot, it must be kept at a temperature above 63°C. It must be used within 2 hours and should not be re-heated after this time.

- Left-over food should be cooled quickly to below 8°C, and then transferred to the refrigerator.

Key terms

High risk food – food that should be stored for only a short amount of time, as it is most likely to cause food poisoning.

Binary fission – dividing process of bacteria.

Food probe – a thermometer that is inserted to check the inside temperature of the food.

Activity

1. Make a list of dos and don'ts in the kitchen to keep food safe to eat.

2. Explain why it is important to regularly check the temperature of your refrigerator.

Check your understanding

1. What conditions do bacteria need to multiply?

2. What is meant by a 'high risk' food?

3. What is the name of the process that bacteria use to divide?

4. What is the temperature danger zone?

5. How can we use the temperature danger zone to control the growth of bacteria?

Exam practice

Bacteria are micro-organisms which cause food spoilage.

a) Name **two** *other* micro-organisms that cause food spoilage. [2]

b) State **three** conditions needed for micro-organisms to grow. [3]

Topic 17: Food poisoning

● **The causes and effects of food poisoning.**

Key terms

Pathogenic bacteria – bacteria that cause illness.

Cross-contamination – the transfer of bacteria between food, equipment or humans.

Many people every year suffer from food poisoning symptoms. It can be caused by poor hygiene and incorrect storage of food. Food poisoning can result in a range of symptoms from stomach cramps to death in more serious cases.

What is the effect of food spoilage?

One of the most serious effects of food spoilage is the contamination of food with harmful bacteria. This causes food poisoning, a common gastrointestinal illness which the Food Standards Agency estimate affects up to 5.5 million people in the UK each year.

Anyone can get food poisoning, but it is especially dangerous for groups of people such as:

● Babies and young children, because their immune (defence) system has not fully developed.

● Pregnant women, because the illness can affect the unborn baby.

● The elderly, because their immune system is weaker.

● People who have an illness or health condition and, as a result, their immune system is weaker.

Food can be contaminated at any stage during production, processing and cooking, and it is important that care is taken to ensure the risk of contamination is kept to a minimum. Bacteria can be transferred by unhygienic food handlers, unclean food preparation areas and not cooking food to a high enough temperature to kill bacteria.

Food poisoning is caused by **pathogenic bacteria**. The most common types of food poisoning in the UK are *Salmonella, E. Coli, Listeria, Staphylococcus aureus* and *Campylobacter.* Other food poisoning bacteria include *Clostridium perfringens* and *Bacillus cereus*.

Below are some of the most common types of food poisoning, their symptoms, incubation time, sources and causes.

Salmonella

Symptoms	Vomiting, diarrhoea, nausea, abdominal pain and fever. Can be serious and in some cases fatal.
Incubation period	2–5 days.
Sources	Raw meat, poultry, eggs, cooked meats and pies, raw unwashed vegetables.
Causes/Control	Cross-contamination and undercooked food.

E coli

Symptoms	Diarrhoea which can be bloody, vomiting and dehydration. Most severe in babies, young children and the elderly. Can lead to kidney failure and death.
Incubation period	2–4 days, but can stay in the intestine for long periods of time.
Sources	Raw meat and poultry, unwashed vegetables, undercooked meat, e.g. burgers.
Causes/Control	Cross-contamination, not cooking food to a high enough temperature.

Listeria

Symptoms	Mild flu-like symptoms to an invasion of the blood system causing septicaemia or meningitis. Can cause stillbirth or miscarriage.
Incubation period	Can take from 5 days to weeks for symptoms to develop.
Sources	Found in manure and soil, unpasteurised milk, soft cheeses and paté, meat and poultry and salad vegetables.
Causes/Control	Thorough cooking and reheating of food can destroy Listeria.

Staphylococcus aureus

Symptoms	Severe vomiting, diarrhoea, and abdominal pains.
Incubation period	2–6 hours, symptoms last no longer than 2 days.
Sources	Found on hands, in the nose and infected cuts, also in foods such as cooked meat and poultry.
Causes/Control	Transferred by unhygienic food handling, hands and droplets in the nose and mouth.

Campylobacter

Symptoms	Diarrhoea, severe abdominal pain, headache, fever and exhaustion.
Incubation period	2–5 days and lasts for the same period.
Sources	Raw meat and undercooked poultry, unpasteurised milk.
Causes/Control	Preventing cross-contamination and thorough cooking of meat can prevent illness.

Bacillus cereus

Symptoms	Diarrhoea and vomiting, abdominal pain.
Incubation period	1–18 hours, lasts for 12–24 hours.
Sources	Rice and rice dishes.
Causes/Control	Avoid reheating rice and cereal dishes as they form spores that can't be destroyed by heat.

Since 1998, all hens producing eggs for selling in the UK are vaccinated against
Salmonella.

What are the causes of food poisoning?

Food poisoning can be caused by:

- Unhygienic preparation of food by food handlers, e.g. unwashed hands.
- Not storing food at the correct temperature, e.g. out on a work surface instead of in the refrigerator.
- Cross-contamination – food being transferred between raw and cooked food, or between food and equipment.
- Using food past its 'use by' date.
- Food is not cooled and refrigerated quickly enough.
- Food is not cooked or re-heated to a high enough temperature.

Cross-contamination

Cross-contamination is a major cause of food poisoning; it is a result of bacteria being transferred from one food to another, from humans, other food or equipment.

It is important to follow a few simple hygiene rules to prevent cross-contamination:

- Wash hands with hot water and soap to remove bacteria.
- Wash all work surfaces before and after cooking to prevent the spread of bacteria.
- Use different colour chopping boards and equipment for different foods, e.g. raw meat on red, vegetables on green.
- Store raw and cooked foods apart, and keep well wrapped to stop bacteria passing from raw food onto cooked.
- Cover food at all times to stop insects or pests getting near the food.
- Use disposable cloths or disinfect cloths regularly to prevent bacteria being spread around the kitchen.
- Empty bins regularly to prevent flies being attracted and then landing on food.

Activity

Read the following article adapted from *The Guardian*, Friday 3 December 2010.

Food poisoning rise linked to undercooked offal

Campylobacter contamination has risen significantly in the last four years after reductions in the early part of the decade.

Consumers have been told to ensure trendy chicken liver dishes have been properly cooked following a worrying rise in food poisoning.

People have been warned by government agencies not to leave pink meat in livers or other offal when they prepare paté or other dishes.

Symptoms include diarrhoea, vomiting, stomach pains and cramps, fever, and generally feeling unwell. They can take up to 10 days to develop and be caused by poor hygiene as well as improperly cooked food.

The food agency said liver, kidneys and other offal should be handled hygienically to avoid cross-contamination and cooked through until 'steaming hot'.

1. What type of food poisoning is the newspaper article describing?

2. What foods caused the food poisoning?

3. What symptoms were experienced?

4. How can this rise in food poisoning be prevented?

Check your understanding

1. Name four types of food poisoning bacteria.

2. List three symptoms of food poisoning.

3. What foods are common sources of food poisoning?

4. What are the most common causes of food poisoning?

5. What is cross-contamination?

6. Give three hygiene rules to prevent cross-contamination.

Exam practice

Explain the importance of colour-coded equipment when handling and preparing food. [4]

Topic 18: Food health, safety and hygiene

What will I learn?

- **How food poisoning can be prevented.**

To prevent food poisoning it is important to have high standards of hygiene and use correct handling techniques when purchasing, storing, preparing and cooking food.

Buying food

When shopping for food it is important to consider the following:

- Look at the 'use by' date to ensure it is in date.
- Buy fresh ingredients such as meat and poultry only when you need them to prevent them going out of date.
- Check that packaging is not damaged or opened.
- Pick up foods for the refrigerator or freezer at the end of the shop to prevent them getting warm or defrosting.
- Pack foods for the freezer together or store in a cool bag or box.
- Avoid leaving food in a warm car, put the food in the coolest part, e.g. boot.
- Pack raw foods separately from cooked food to prevent cross-contamination.
- Unpack refrigerator and freezer food as quickly as possible when you get home to keep it as cool as possible.

Storing food

Food can be stored in the refrigerator, freezer or at an **ambient temperature** in a food cupboard. It is important to check the dates on foods regularly and use the food with the shortest date first. Food that is out of date should be thrown away.

The following rules are important when storing food:

- Perishable food should be stored in the refrigerator at 0°C to 5°C.
- Frozen food should be stored at –18°C.
- Food should be kept covered to prevent cross-contamination.
- Do not put warm food into the fridge, cool it down quickly and then store.
- Cooked foods should be kept above raw foods in the refrigerator.
- Don't overload the fridge.
- Don't refreeze food once it has defrosted.
- Use stock rotation when storing foods in a food cupboard, keep dried and tinned food in a cool, dry place, away from any pets or pests.

Key Term

Ambient temperature – room temperature.

Preparing food

It is important during the preparation of food that it is kept out of the temperature danger zone for as long as possible and that food handlers follow the personal hygiene rules below:

- Wash hands thoroughly with antibacterial soap and hot water before handling food, after handling raw meat, emptying rubbish bins and visiting the toilet.
- Tie back long hair or cover it with a hair net.
- Wear a clean apron or overall to prepare food.
- Keep nails short and clean, and remove jewellery, especially rings.
- Don't cough or sneeze over food, and avoid working with food if feeling unwell.
- Cover cuts with a blue plaster.

As well as displaying good personal hygiene it is important that food preparation areas are clean and hygienic. This can be ensured by:

- Cleaning work surfaces before and after cooking with an antibacterial cleaning product.
- Cleaning the sink and cooker at the end of a cooking session.
- Preparing raw and cooked foods on different chopping boards to avoid cross-contamination.
- Covering foods to prevent contamination from flies.
- Keeping equipment clean.
- Washing and sterilising dish cloths and tea towels frequently.

Cooking and reheating food

Thorough cooking of food is essential to kill bacteria. If food is not heated to a high enough temperature for a long enough time, food poisoning can occur. To prevent this, the following rules should be followed when cooking food:

- Cook food to at least 72°C for 2 minutes, this should be the temperature at the centre of the food and it can be checked using a temperature probe.
- Serve food quickly after it has been cooked to prevent it being left at a temperature suitable for bacterial growth.
- If you are keeping food hot before serving, keep it at 63°C or above.
- Food that is going to be re-heated should be cooled quickly, covered and transferred to the refrigerator.
- Food should be re-heated only once, and it should be heated to 72°C for 2 minutes.
- If you are re-heating food in a microwave you should stir it frequently to avoid cold spots, and it can be tested with a food probe to check the correct temperature has been achieved.

Check core temperatures with a food temperature probe

Activities

'Scientific evidence shows that simple and good hygiene practices can reduce the risk of illness and infection at home and in the community.'

BBC News bulletin 2007

1. Describe the simple and good hygiene practices that need to be followed and explain why they reduce the risk of food poisoning.

2. Produce a poster to display in your school kitchen to show younger pupils the personal hygiene rules they should follow when handling food.

Check your understanding

1. List three rules that should be followed when buying food. Give a reason why you think each is important.

2. State the correct temperature for:

   a) A refrigerator

   b) A freezer.

3. Suggest three ways that food can be stored safely to prevent the growth of bacteria.

4. Give two rules for safe re-heating of foods.

Exam practice

1. Kris is preparing the following family meal:

   Thai chicken curry with rice

   Chocolate mousse

   Give advice to Kris on how the high risk foods should be **prepared** and **cooked** to avoid food poisoning. [8]

2. Assess the importance of practising a high standard of food hygiene in the home when:

   a) Buying and storing food.

   b) Preparing and cooking food. [10]

Topic 19: Food legislation and regulations

There is a range of legislation (laws and acts) in place that ensures food hygiene standards are maintained in food preparation, manufacture and retail premises. This legislation is enforced by statutory agencies such as the Environmental Health Department and the Food Standards Agency.

Food Safety Act 1990

The key requirements of the Act are that food must comply with food safety requirements, must be 'of the nature, substance and quality demanded', and must be correctly described (labelled).

The main responsibilities for all food businesses under the Act are:

- To ensure you do not include anything in food, remove anything from food or treat food in any way which means it would be damaging to the health of people eating it.
- To ensure that the food you serve or sell is of the nature, substance or quality which consumers would expect.
- To ensure that the food is labelled, advertised and presented in a way that is not false or misleading.

Food Safety (General Food Hygiene) Regulations (1995)

The Food Safety (General Food Hygiene) Regulations (1995) set out basic food hygiene standards that apply across the European Community as part of the Food Hygiene Directive (93/43/EC). These affect the whole food chain – from the farm to the shop or the restaurant. Each 'food preparation premises' must be registered with the Local Authority, where environmental health officers ensure that correct procedures and standards are being followed.

Food Hygiene Rating (Wales) Act 2013

The Welsh Assembly's Food Hygiene Rating (Wales) Act 2013 will see Wales become the first country in the UK to introduce a mandatory scheme requiring food businesses to openly display their hygiene rating. This scheme is based on the FSA's voluntary food hygiene rating scheme.

The Act will require food businesses to display their food hygiene rating – from 0 (urgent improvement necessary) to 5 (very good), based on their compliance with food law requirements – and local authorities to enforce the mandatory scheme in their area and ensure ratings are correctly displayed. It is expected the mandatory scheme will come into operation later this year to allow businesses time to prepare.

Environmental Health Officers

Environmental Health Officers are responsible for carrying out measures for protecting public health, including administering and enforcing legislation related to environmental health and providing support to minimise health and safety hazards.

They are responsible for the following:

- Inspecting food facilities to check temperatures and equipment.
- Taking samples of food products for testing.
- Hygiene of food handlers and kitchens.
- Checking that HACCP procedures are being followed.

If they find any issues during a routine visit they can advise on changes needed, and, where necessary, have the authority to close premises down. They also involved in investigating public health nuisances, and implementing disease control.

Their role is focused on prevention, consultation, investigation, and education of the community regarding health risks and maintaining a safe environment.

Food Standards Agency (FSA)

The Food Standards Agency is responsible for food safety and food hygiene across the UK. The FSA works with local authorities to enforce food safety regulations and has staff who work in UK meat plants to check that the requirements of the regulations are being met.

Their aims are to ensure:

- Foods produced or sold in the UK are safe to eat.
- Imported food is safe to eat.
- Food producers and caterers give priority to consumer interests in relation to food.
- Consumers have the information and understanding they need to make informed choices about where and what they eat.
- Regulation is effective, risk-based and proportionate, is clear about the responsibilities of food business operators, and protects consumers and their interests from fraud and other risks.
- Enforcement is effective, consistent, risk-based and proportionate and is focused on improving public health.

Stretch and challenge

1. Find out more about the Food Hygiene Rating (Wales) Act 2013.

   Discuss whether you think that it is a good idea to introduce this system.

2. Extend your knowledge of food poisoning bacteria by looking on the Internet for more articles about outbreaks.

   Using the articles identify the cause of the outbreak, the effects and suggest ways further outbreaks could be prevented.

3. Find out about a special mould called mycoprotein, used to make a high protein vegetarian food called Quorn. List recipes where Quorn is used as a main ingredient.

4. Some vegetables are blanched before they are frozen. Find out what this process means and explain why it is carried out.

Exam practice

Describe the role of the Environmental Health Department in the monitoring of food hygiene standards. [4]

Controlled Assessment

Controlled Assessment: What is it?

Controlled Assessment used to be called Coursework. It is now a school-based task that can only be completed under supervision from your teacher.

60% of your GCSE in Home Economics Food and Nutrition comes from Controlled Assessment tasks. You will complete two tasks:

Task 1 is worth 20% of your GCSE

Task 2 is worth 40% of your GCSE

You will complete Task 1 towards the end of year 10, and Task 2 during year 11.

Tasks change regularly, and your teacher will give you guidance on the tasks you need to complete. You will also be provided with a page and time limit to complete the tasks. It is important that you are aware of the criteria before you start.

What will I do in Controlled Assessment?

There are four main sections to your Controlled Assessment task, these are as follows.

Investigation and research

This involves looking in detail at your chosen area and gathering information that will help you to understand the topic better. You will also look for recipe ideas and think of ways to make them suitable for the task.

Planning

This section is about organisation. You will need to plan what you need to make your dishes, including ingredients and equipment, and you will have to think about the order in which you will cook your dishes to make the best use of your time.

Production of dishes

Here you will be marked on your actual cooking, you need to be calm and confident, choose dishes that show a range of skills and make sure your dishes are presented to a high standard.

Evaluation

It's always important to look back on your work and think about what you could have improved. This doesn't mean that you performed badly but it gives you an opportunity to make your work even better. You will need to think about sensory analysis, nutritional analysis and cost in this section, too.

Task 1

Task 1 will be marked as follows:

- Investigation and planning (12 marks)
- Production (20 marks)
- Evaluation (8 marks).

There is a **limit of 8 sides of A4** for the investigation and planning, and evaluation sections of Task 1.

You should not spend more than 10 hours completing this task, this includes the cooking of the dishes and time will be logged on a record sheet.

Investigation and planning

To get the best marks in this section it is important to show that you have investigated the chosen topic in detail so that you can make informed choices about the dishes you will prepare for the practical.

This section should include:

- **Key words** – these should be highlighted from the brief and a definition given that shows understanding.
- **Analysis of the task** – say what you have been asked to do and what information you are going to look at in the investigation.
- **Secondary research** into the topic, this could be from books, the Internet or magazines and newspapers. (See page 164.)
- **Primary research** into the topic can take the form of a survey, questionnaire or a tasting session. (See page 163.)
- **Set criteria or aims** – these could include reference to your skills, healthy eating guidelines, cost, availability of ingredients, special diets, etc. Check that you have considered the key words in your aims.
- **Suggest possible dishes** – think of about eight dishes, try and think of a variety of savoury and sweet dishes, say why they would be suitable ideas, refer back to the criteria or aims.
- **Reasons for choice** – choose the four dishes that you are going to make and say why you have chosen them.
- **Production plan** – produce a plan for making (see page 169), this should include time, preparation and hygiene and safety points.

Production

In this section you will be assessed on the practical skills shown, you need to show that you are able to:

- Organise yourself during the practical session by following your production plan.
- Demonstrate a wide range of food handling and preparation skills.
- Work safely and hygienically.
- Use equipment efficiently.
- Present your dishes with a high quality finish.

You need to make sure that you have photographs of all your finished dishes.

Evaluation

In this section you will need to evaluate at least one of the dishes* that you have made, you will need to comment on:

- **Nutritional analysis** – what nutrients the dish provides, what foods provide these nutrients and whether it meets the guideline daily amounts.

- **Sensory analysis** – you could use a star profile to highlight the important sensory qualities of the food and comment on taste, texture and appearance.

- **Cost** – calculate the cost of making the whole recipe, and the cost per serving. Comment on whether it is good value for money, you could even make suggestions for ways you could reduce the cost.

Give an overall evaluation of your work; refer back to your aims to identify whether you have achieved what you set out to do, give suggestions for any improvements you would make if you were to complete the task again.

> * Students are encouraged to produce at least two of their dishes in one session and should evaluate those two dishes. This is considered to be good practice and excellent preparation for completing Task 2.

Task 2

Task 2 will be marked as follows:

- Investigation/Research (10 marks)
- Planning – development and selecting ideas, plan of action (15 marks)
- Production (45 marks)
- Evaluation (10 marks).

There is a limit of **8 sides of A3 or 16 sides of A4** for the Investigation/Research, Planning and Evaluation sections of Task 2.

You should not spend more than 20 hours completing this task, this includes the cooking of the dishes and time will be logged on a record sheet.

Investigation/Research

In this section it is important that you investigate as much about your chosen topic as possible. Try to find information from a wide range of sources and record where the information was from. Comment on the information you have gathered and present the work in your own words. Your work in this section should cover **two sides of A3 paper** and include both text and images.

It is important to include the following information on pages 1 and 2:

- **The Task title**
- **An explanation of the task** – write a paragraph explaining what the brief is asking you to do in your own words.
- **Key words** – chose the relevant key words from the task title and explain what they mean. This can be presented as a mind map or list.
- **Aims** – you need to bullet point the main aims you hope to achieve when carrying out this task, e.g. I aim to investigate children's diets by researching on the Internet, carrying out analysis on products available for children and producing a questionnaire to ask parents of 3–5-year-old children.
- **Research analysis** – select a range of relevant information using both primary and secondary sources to show you have researched the topic thoroughly.

- **Research analysis** – once you have carried out your research, you will need to summarise your main findings and suggest how this information is going to help you produce and develop ideas to meet the brief.

Planning – developing and selecting ideas, plan of action

In this section you will consider a range of dishes that you could make to suit the task, and carry out development work to help you decide on the four dishes you will make in your final practical. This section of the task should be completed over **three pages of A3**.

It is important that the following information is included in this section:

- **Criteria** – it is important that you are clear on what you are hoping to achieve when you are deciding on which dishes to choose for your practical work. Setting criteria is helpful in allowing you to check that the dishes you have chosen are suitable and meet the aims of the task. Criteria for selecting dishes can be based on a variety of factors such as nutritional needs, appearance or cost. For example, if completing a task on diets for children, one specification point may say:

  I must include dishes that are high in calcium as this mineral is important for strong bones and teeth in children.

- **Mind map of ideas** – research a selection of ideas that meet the brief, try to include at least 10 ideas, ensure they are varied and would show a range of practical skills.

- **Practical recipe trials** – you should carry out three recipe trials to allow you to trial and develop some of the ideas that you think would be most suitable.
  E.g. If you were developing a main meal that should encourage people to eat more fruit and vegetables, you may trial three pies that include different vegetables in each filling and carry out sensory analysis to find out which was the most popular. Your experimental work should link directly to the topic and should be supported by sensory analysis and you need to write conclusions from your results.
  When you are carrying out your trials, you can make smaller quantities of the recipes to reduce the cost.
  You should aim to complete the practical trials in three hours.

- **Criteria chart** – to ensure you choose to make the most suitable dishes, you will need to compare your 8–10 initial ideas against the criteria or specifications that you set. The four dishes that that score the highest or meet the most specification points will be the dishes that you will make.

- **Reasons for choice** – once you have selected your four ideas you need to give detailed reasons for why they are the most suitable.
  E.g. I have chosen to make pizza pockets for a children's lunchtime snack as I can hide lots of vegetables in the tomato sauce inside the pizza, and I can use half wholemeal and half white flour to make the bread dough, which will meet my specification to make it higher in fibre.

- **Production plan** – it is very important that you produce a detailed plan that you can follow when completing your practical work. When you carry out your practical work, it is necessary for you to make at least two dishes in each cooking session. Your planning should reflect this, to show that you are able to sequence the making of your dishes.

For example, you may start by preparing bread dough, but then make a cake whilst the dough is proving, then shape and cook the pizza and finish off by decorating the cake.

You should not write out each dish as separate recipes, this page should also include ingredients (with quantities), an equipment list and hygiene and safety points included on the step-by-step plan.

Production

This section is worth the highest amount of marks in Task 2, it is important that you have chosen dishes with a range of skills.

You also need to ensure that you have demonstrated:

- Adequate planning, showing organisation of yourself, ingredients and the work area.
- Attention to health and safety.
- An ability to use equipment effectively and efficiently.
- An ability to work independently.
- An ability to follow the order of work.
- That you can complete the task on time.
- Good presentation skills, with attention to finish and quality.

Evaluation

In this section you will need to reflect on both your written task and your practical work, your evaluation will need to include the following:

- Annotated photographs of the dishes made.
- Reference to the original aims set, and whether or not you met them.
- Comments on the planning of work, meeting set deadlines and planning for the practical session.
- Comments on how useful your research and experimental work was.
- Nutritional analysis, sensory analysis and costing, with conclusions stating what you found out.
- A discussion of the strengths and weaknesses of the whole task (not just the practical work).
- Ways in which you would improve your project and ways you could develop your work further.

Your work in this section should be **two pages of A3 paper** and should include text, sensory charts and photographs.

To help you get a clearer understanding of what needs to be included in your Controlled Assessment tasks, look at the examples of Task 1 and Task 2 over the following pages. There are helpful comments and tips that will ensure you provide all the vital information to allow you to get the best result.

Task 1

Protein foods can be an **expensive** item on shopping list. Explore and produce **four** protein dishes that can be both interesting and economical.

Show which task you have chosen and highlight the key words to help focus your research.

Explain why you've chosen this topic and what you hope to gain from it.

Introduction

    I have chosen this brief because I know that protein is a **vital nutrient** in our diet for growth, repair and as a secondary source of energy. Also because I know that the cost of protein foods are rising, so I want to find cheaper foods that still contain protein, that can be available for everyone so they can get the right nutrients and have a healthy diet.

Key Words

- **Protein foods**- All types of food, but must be high in protein.
- **Economical**- Cheaper to buy and available to people on a small income.
- **Interesting**- Food that looks appetising and has a good flavour to it.

Analysis

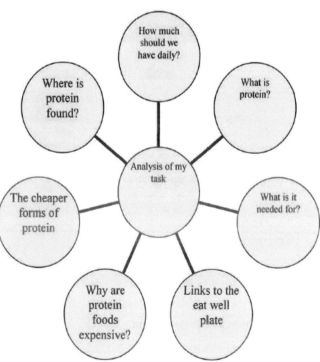

Produce clear aims that will focus your research. Make your aims specific and relevant to the brief.

Aims

- To conduct research on cheaper forms of protein food
- To complete a questionnaire on the types of proteins eat and compare 2 dishes on price and nutrition value
- Use my findings of my questionnaire to produce a specification for my practical.
- Make a list a suitable recipes for cheaper protein foods
- Select four dishes and reject some and give reason for this
- Produce a time plan for my practical
- Carry out my practical work
- Evaluate my practical work by looking at the sensory qualities, nutritional value and the cost

Limitations

For this task I only have **10 hours** to complete both my written and practical work. My written work must only cover **6 A4 pages** that are typed up. I must also consider the cost of my ingredients, how long each dish takes to cook and the space in the oven.

Secondary Research

Task 1 is a maximum of 8 pages of A4.

Protein is an **important** is required in the body for growth and maintenance. It's sometimes used for energy as a secondary source. The eatwell plate shows us that we need a good amount of protein. The amount of protein you should have depends on your age, size and how active you are. Some say at least 15% of total calories should come from protein.

Protein foods are foods that are high in protein. There are two sources of protein foods; **animals and plants**. Animal proteins come from or are the products of animals. These include meat, fish, poultry, eggs, milk and cheese. These sources contain a full range of essential amino acids that are needed in the diet and are have **High Biological value**. The plant sources are foods such as quorn, nuts, pulses (peas, beans and lentils), rice and cereals. These foods have **Low Biological value** because they lack one or more of the amino acids.

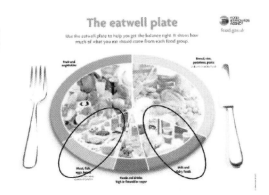

The eatwell plate

As the price of meat is rising, many people are looking for less expensive foods that are still high in protein. There are many cheaper cuts of meat out there, for example instead of chicken breast there is chicken thighs or wings. In some supermarkets they do a basics range, which is cheaper, but still provides us with protein. For example basics mince beef is 96p instead of £2.87.

For fish you could buy tinned fish instead of fresh because it's cheaper. Or you could just chose a cheaper fresh fish like Coley and Tout.

However, most cheap protein foods are from plants. These foods still provide the nutrients and taste good too. Eggs are another cheap protein food that can be cooked in many different ways. Nuts and pulses are also cheap and contain a high value of protein. There are many different alternatives. Even in all the supermarkets, the prices tell you that plant sources or cheaper than animal sources at providing protein. For example eggs, which are an animal source, cost 69p for six, on the other hand chicken breast, which is an animal source, can cost £6.00. Both are a good source of protein but by buying eggs you can save yourself £4.31.

Relevant and concise research, explain how this will help you decide what dishes to make and link it to reasons for choice to gain the highest marks.

Primary Research

For my primary research I made a questionnaire. The answers that the majority chose are in red.

1. Do you think protein is an important nutrient in your diet? Yes No
2. How many protein foods do you consume per day? 1-3 4-7 8+
3. How much per week do you spend on protein foods? £1-£5 £6-10 £10-15 £16+
4. Would you say protein foods are expensive? Yes No
5. Do you think you eat enough protein? Yes No Not sure
6. What protein foods do you mostly eat? Eggs Cheese Chicken Beef

The Results

From the results from my questionnaire, I have found out that people know that protein is an important nutrient in their diet. Most people do eat a fair amount of protein foods per day, so they are getting enough. Also that most do spend a lot on proteins a week and find them expensive. Most of them didn't know if they were eating enough and people mostly eat Chicken, which can be very

Primary research is useful for finding out opinions, make sure you use your findings to make decisions.

will make dishes that are going to be cheap to make, so they wont be les with other types of protein food instead of chicken, so they can see that other foods are as good as chicken in providing protein to their diet. To make sure that they get enough protein I will do dishes that are high in protein so they know that they are getting enough in their diet.

Other primary research could be carried out such as tasting sessions, product analysis and experimental work.

Practical
Design Specifications

- Should be suitable for my subject of using cheaper protein foods.
- If so, follow the healthy eating guidelines
- Contain nutrients from all the groups
- Show a variety of different skills
- Contain a mixture of colours, shapes and textures
- Be a mixture of sweet and savoury dishes
- Have a contrast of temperatures

Avoid use of the term 'design specification' as it is a term specific to Food Technology not Food & Nutrition.

Detailed criteria or aims will allow you to build a clear picture of what you hope to achieve in your practical work.

Possible dishes

I have chosen 8 possible dishes that all use cheaper forms of protein. I have rejected 4 and chosen 4 that I think are better to do.

- **Carrot and Lentil soup**. I have **chosen** this dish because lentils are a cheap form of protein and also carrots will contribute to one of your five a day. Also because it cheap and shows a different alternative to meat.
- **Quiche.** I have **chosen** this dish because you use eggs, milk and cheese which all have protein in, and are relatively cheap and it has lots of vegetables in it.
- **Sweet and sour chicken with egg fried rice**-using chicken thighs instead of breast. I have **rejected** this dish because it doesn't contain that much protein and the flavouring are expensive.
- **Chicken Curry**-using chicken thighs instead of breast again. I have **rejected** this dish, because I feel it's not as good as the others and I want to show alternatives to chicken.
- **Spaghetti Bolognese** -using mince meat. I have **chosen** this dish because mince meat is a cheap form of protein.
- **Fruit salad with Greek yogurt and nuts.** I have **rejected** this dish, because I feel it doesn't show enough skills when making it and that it didn't provide enough protein to make it a high in protein dish.
- **Tuna and Sweetcorn Pizza**. I have **chosen** this because tinned tuna is a cheap protein food and the sweetcorn and peppers will give you one of your five a day, so the dish is balanced in nutrients.

Refer back to the task, any skills that you will show and whether the dishes meet your criteria, try to be as specific as possible.

Qualify your reasons for choice, showing how the dishes meet your brief; use your research results here too.

Reasons for choice

Quiche- I have chosen this dish because it contains eggs, milk and cheese which are all protein foods and are all relatively cheap, so therefore they fit into my brief. The quiche shows a variety of skills, including making shortcrust pastry, and because I'm doing a Mediterranean quiche its will show preparation of vegetables. The dish is balanced with nutrients. There is protein in the eggs, milk and cheese for growth and repair. Milk and cheese also provide fat for warmth and protection of internal organs, but also have calcium for growth and for strong bones and teeth. The vegetable in it are a good source of fibre which assists with the removal of waste, and also contribute to one of your five a day. The pastry provides you with starch for energy. To make it healthier I could use skimmed milk and low fat cheese. The dish has a variety of colours with the vegetables in. However to make it more colourful I will serve it with a green salad. This would also make a contrast in temperatures.

Carrot and Lentil Soup- I have chosen this dish because it contains lentils which have protein in and are cheap, so it fits into my brief. The soup shows some skills such as vegetable preparation and the use of a blender. The soup is balanced with nutrients, such as protein which comes from the lentils. The lentils also will provide you with energy and is also an excellent source of fibre.. The carrots will provide some fibre to the dish. The dish is also low in fat to fit into the healthy eating guidelines. To make a variety of temperatures I can serve the soup with a bread roll. This would also balance the dish by providing starch for energy.

Bolognese- I have chosen this dish because it contain mince meat, which is a cheap form of protein and the cheese so its fits into my brief. The Bolognese shows the skill of meat preparation. The dish is balance in nutrients. The minced meat contains protein and a little fat. The pasta contains starch for energy. To make a contrast in colour I will serve the Spaghetti Bolognese with a little bit a grated parmesan cheese. This would also add a dairy product to the dish for fat and strong bones and teeth.

Pizza- I have chosen this dish because it contains cheese, which is a protein food and provides calcium for strong bones and teeth. Also because for the topping I will use tuna, sweetcorn and onions. The tuna will be tinned, so therefore it will be a cheaper form of protein than fresh tuna. The sweetcorn is one of your five a day and contain minerals, vitamins and fibre. The base of the pizza will contain starch, so will provide you with energy. I will garnish the dish with rocket at the end, so this will give the dish a contrast of temperature and colour.

Show the time you will start each stage of making.

Time Plan

Time	Method	Points
9:00am	Preparation time: • Prepare self-hair, apron, wash hands • Place ingredients on white trays • Collect equipment- hand blender. • Turn on oven 220'C • Collect washing up equipment • Grease tins for bread and pizza • Open tins and grate cheese	
9:20am	Bread/Pizza base: Make dough, knead for 10mins, shape into 6 rolls and leave some for pizza base, leave to rise in grill until double in size	Use tepid water Place in warm place to rise
9:35	Clear and wash up.	Use hot soapy water.

Highlight the dish you are making.

Time	Task	Safety / Notes
9:40	**Meat sauce**: Prepare the meat sauce for Bolognese- peel and chop up onions, cooked meat and onions and add tomatoes. Flavour to taste and leave to simmer for 20-25 minutes or until meat and tomatoes or cooked.	Pan handle over work top. Use a clean spoon to taste with. Be careful with sharp knife.
10:00	**Soup**: Leave lentils to cook in the stock and milk with cumin seed and chilli flakes for 20-25 minutes. Check on **bread**, if it has raised put in oven for 15 minutes or until browned at 220'C	Place pan handle over work top. Keep heat on low so lentils cook slowly.
10:15	Clear and wash up	Use hot soapy water.
10:20	**Quiche**: Make shortcrust pastry using rubbing in method, roll out and line dish and prepare vegetables and filling. Put in oven for 25-30 minutes at 200'C or until pastry is cooked and egg has set.	Use cold water for pastry. Use oven gloves when putting in oven. Take care with Sharp knife.
	Clear and wash up	Use hot soapy water
	Check if **bread** is cooked and sounds hollow inside	Use oven gloves to take bread out of oven. Place on cooling tray.
10:30	**Soup**: Add carrots (cut up using food processor) to the soup and leave to simmer.	Use food processors for carrots before adding
	Clear and wash up food processor.	Use hot soapy water **and take** ...th blades.
10:40	**Pizza**: Shape out base ... re with sharp knives and oven for 15 minutes at ... n gloves to put in oven.	
11:50	**Quiche**-Check if cooke... oven gloves to take out of oven. **Place on cooling tray.**	
	Clear and wash up	Use hot soapy water
10:55	**Pasta**: Cook pasta for Bolognese in boiling water for 10-12 minutes or until pasta is al dente.	Make sure the water has boiled before adding the pasta **and** place the pan handle over the work top.
11:00	**Soup**: Check if cooked, and then blend the soup and then leave on hop to stay warm.	Take care with blender; keep wires out of the way.
11:05	Clear and wash up	Take care when washing up blades **and** use hot soapy water.
11:10	**Pizza**- Take out the oven and put on plate to serve	Use oven gloves.
	Pasta- When cooked drain the pasta and put on a plate.	Take care with boiling water
	Switch off oven	
11:20	**Serve all dishes**-if soup not hot enough, warm in microwave. Place in bowl. Bread rolls on a plate. Spaghetti Bolognese on a plate with grated parmesan on top to garnish. Quiche on a plate served with a green salad and tomatoes. Pizza on a plate, garnish of rocket.	Label the dishes
	Clear and wash up	Use hot soapy water.

Show that you are aware of the need to clean as you go by adding time for cleaning up during making.

Highlight any important safety points.

> Your evaluation should link back to the brief, it is important to comment on the sensory qualities, costing and nutritional information. You won't achieve the higher marks without analysis.

Evaluation

My practical went really well, I managed to make all my four dishes in the time provided and wash up my equipment. The dish that I have decided to evaluate for the four I made is the Mediterranean Quiche, because I feel that it's the best dish that fitted my brief. I will evaluate sensory analysis, how my dish looked and tasted, the cost to see how economical it is or how I could make it more economical and I will also nutritionally analyse the dish.

Sensory Analysis

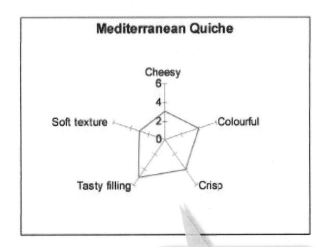

> Star charts are a clear way to show the sensory qualities of your dish.

I asked my family to taste the Mediterranean Quiche and give it a mark out of 5 on a number of qualities. I then put the results of this in a star profile. I can see their views on the table quite clearly. The Quiche had a tasty filling and was colourful and the pastry crisp. To make the quiche better I could have added more cheese to get a more cheesy flavouring. Also to get a softer texture I could have taken it out of the oven earlier so the filling didn't set as much. I served the quiche with a green salad and some cherry tomatoes to add a contrast in temperature, colour and to add some nutrients such as minerals. The salad would also give them one of their five a day.

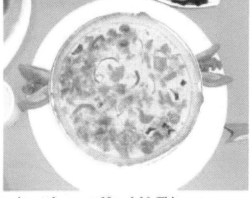

Cost Analysis

Cost recipe: £2.37
Cost portion: £0.39
Cost for 100g: £0.25

I used the Jenny Ridgewell Nutritional Program to work out the costing and the nutritional content of my quiche. As you can see above the costing of the Quiche was economical, because it was only 39p per portion for a good quality and size. If you want to a restaurant it would have cost at least £8 or even more. The whole quiche only cost £2.37 to make. When I compare this price to one from a supermarket, which was the same quality and size, it cost between £5 and £6. This means you are saving £3-£4. The reason why the cost was low was because I used the cheap forms of protein like eggs which only cost 69p for six and cheap vegetables.

Nutrition Information

Nutrition information	per 100g	per portion	GDA (women)	GDA (men)	GDA (5-18 yr)	traffic light
Energy	180.6 kcal	283.5 kcal	14.1%	11.3%	15.7%	
Protein	6.2 g	9.8 g	21.8%	17.8%	40.9%	
Carbohydrate*	12.9 g	20.3 g	8.8%	6.7%	9.2%	
Starch*	9.8 g	15.5 g				
Fat	11.8 g	18.6 g	26.6%	19.6%	26.6%	
Saturated Fat*	5.4 g	8.6 g	43.1%	28.7%	43.1%	

Protein

This nutrition analysis shows that the quiche is quite low in calories and carbohydrates, which is good; however the quiche is high in fat and Saturated fat (this can lead to high cholesterol). It was probably from the pastry. It provides us with starch, which would give use energy. I served the quiche with a green salad amd peppers; therefore this would add fibre, vitamin A & C and iron to the dish. It would also give the dish a contrast in temperature and colour. From the bar chart before you can see that my quiche was high in protein, so therefore it was a good dish to make to fit into my brief. The ingredients that contained protein were eggs, milk and cheese. All the dishes I cooked managed to fit into my brief, as they were all cheap to make using the cheaper forms of protein.

> Link back to the task and say how you met your aims. It is important to also suggest areas for improvement and further development.

How my aims were met

I chose to investigate the cheaper sources of protein. I fulfilled the aims that I set myself for my investigation. I fulfilled them by:

- Researching the sources of protein foods and their costs. I found that there are two sources; animal and plant. The animal one was more expensive, but there are cheap cuts of meats that you can buy and also products of animals such as eggs and milk. Vegetable sources tend to be cheaper. Pulses are relatively inexpensive and I used lentils in my soup.
- Carrying out a questionnaire to find out which how much protein foods people ate and which ones and if they found them expensive. I found that most ate a considerably amount of protein and they ate chicken most. Also that most, if not all found protein foods expensive.
- Using the information I found to come up with suitable dishes for my practical.
- Cooking 4 dishes showing the cheaper forms of protein foods. My dishes were Mediterranean Quiche, Pizza, Carrot and Lentil soup and Spaghetti Bolognese.
- Evaluating one of the dishes that I made during my practical. That dish was the Mediterranean Quiche.

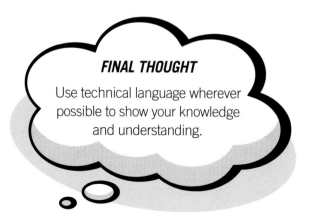

> **FINAL THOUGHT**
> Use technical language wherever possible to show your knowledge and understanding.

Task 2

> Research on this page is focused and constantly applies to the task.

Healthy Food for Children – Page 1

BRIEF

Parents are encouraged to provide healthier options of food and drink for their children.

AIMS

- I aim to select an age group and suitable event that will help promote healthier options.
- I aim to complete secondary research on the internet and in books.
- I aim to collect primary research such as questionnaires, surveys and to disassemble products
- I aim to select dishes that include the correct amount of protein, calcium, iron and carbohydrate for a child.
- I aim to make the dishes using a variety of skills and that are suitable for the brief.
- I aim to make my dishes quick and do not need any special equipment or skills so that I can make my dishes and therefore feed their children healthily.
- I finally aim to evaluate my work.

> Some general aims, but are most are specific and link successfully to the brief.

RESEARCH TYPES

Secondary Research: I will use internet, books, and magazines as they offer a wide variety of statistics, facts and information related to my brief. The websites I have used are:

SOURCE A: http://www.nhs.uk/change4life/Pages/change-for-life.aspx

SOURCE B: www.schoolfoodtrust.org.uk

SOURCE C: www.healthystart.nhs.uk

SOURCE C: http://www.eatwell.gov.uk/foodlabels/trafficlights/

SOURCE D: http://www.nhs.uk/change4life/Pages/change-for-life.aspx

SOURCE E: http://www.bbc.co.uk/cbeebies/icancook/

SOURCE F: http://health.marksandspencer.com/our-health-ranges/simply-kids

Primary Research: I am going to disassemble suitable party food products that are suitable for an age group of 4 to 9 years old. I will disassemble six types of sausage rolls, as this is the food I hope to make. I am going to disassemble products to compare the nutritional content as I can then adapt my dishes. Also this will help me find out supermarket prices, quality and who has the healthier foods. I will also ask a parent to provide me with a food diary of their child, analyse their results and comment on how they can adapt their diet.

KEYWORDS

Packed lunches, healthy, Government schemes, presentation, breakfast, finger foods, party foods, family portions, change4life, advertising, colourful, vitamins, minerals, events, schools, Cardiff Council, colourful plates, traffic light Jamie Oliver and Annabelle Karmel, nutrients.

> Key words should come directly from the brief and include a definition to show understanding.

SECONDARY RESEARCH:

Parents are encouraged, in many ways to feed their children healthy foods and drinks. The following research shows ways in which the parents are encouraged.

The Government decided to ban junk food adverts being shown on television to young children. In January 2008, the Government decided to do this because they are not being nagged by their children to buy the foods they see advertised. The new rule means adverts for food and drinks high in fat, salt or sugar cannot be broadcast around shows aimed at four to nine-year-olds. (Source A)

Celebrities such as Jamie Oliver and Annabel Karmel, encourage parents to feed their children healthy, quick and cheap food and drink by providing parents with recipe ideas through their shows. They then have knowledge about how to feed their children more healthily.

After looking at the research, the GDA for a child is not, as you would expect, half of the GDA for an adult. An adult female needs 2000 kcal a day where as a female five to ten year old needs 1800 kcal. The child needs energy as they are very active and are growing. An adult needs 45g and a child needs 24g of protein. Protein is required for growth and repair. Good sources for protein include fish, eggs and meat. Although calcium is not in the table to the right, a child needs 450mg of calcium and an adult needs 700mg. Children need calcium in order to have healthy bones and teeth. Sources of calcium include milk, yoghurt and cheese, which is easy to eat. Children therefore need vitamin D which is vital for the absorption of calcium and sources of vitamin D are margarine and cereals. Iron is also needed for the formation of red blood cells and a child needs 6.5mg. A great source of iron is red meat, although this is hard to eat for children. Vitamin C is vital for the absorption of iron and sources of vitamin C include citrus fruits such as lemons and oranges. I need to search for recipes that include a high amount of protein, iron, calcium and carbohydrates for energy. I will try and choose dishes that have all these nutrients so that the parents will be feeding their children healthier.

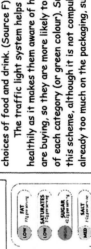

NUTRITION		GDA
Fat		
Sugar		

> Age-specific nutritional data is very useful; this can be used for comparison during development work when developing and evaluating.

The traffic light system helps parents to decide which food is healthy as it makes them aware of how much fat, sugar and salt they are buying, so they are more likely to look around for the lower amount of each category (or green colour). Supermarkets such as the Government decided this scheme, although it is not compulsory on the packaging, such as the barcode and logo. (Source F)

Healthy Foods For Children – Page 2

Energy Sources

- Carbohydrate
- Protein
- Fat

Major Constituents

- Water
- Starch
- Englyst fibre
- Fat
- Total sugars
- Protein

Vitamins (100%)

- Folate
- Niacin
- Pantothenate
- Riboflavin
- Thiamin
- Vitamin A
- Vitamin B12
- Vitamin B6
- Vitamin C
- Vitamin D
- Vitamin E

Minerals, Protein & Energy (100%)

- Calcium
- Copper
- Iodine
- Iron
- Magnesium
- Phosphorus
- Potassium
- Sodium
- Zinc
- Protein
- Energy

Marks and Spencer's birthday party platter (see picture above)

Secondary research should be a summary of the information you have found on your chosen topic. The research in this example is clear and concise whilst covering a range of nutritional information and influences on diet.

From the results I can see that the child is having too little carbohydrate and too much fat. The recommended daily amounts are 60% and 35% respectively. The child is having more than enough carbohydrate, although she is not consuming any vitamin D so she may have rickets. A deficiency in calcium causes rickets, which is on the rise in the UK. She is also having just enough iron and enough vitamin C, which helps absorb the iron. Iron is needed for healthy blood cells. If she consumes any less than this it could cause her to develop anaemia so she should eat more cereals and red meat. The analysis shows that the child is having too much salt. Advice for the parents would be to add less salt to their foods as too much salt can lead to nerve and brain damage which can eventually lead to death.

I would recommend that the child should eat more breakfast cereals which are fortified with Vitamin D. I would also suggest that the child eats more nuts such as hazel nuts and Brazil nuts that contain vitamin E as the child is slightly deficient in this micronutrient. I would also suggest that the child has more carbohydrates so you could replace one of the meals with a pasta dish. I would also make sure that the child keeps high fat foods to the minimum as she is having too much fat. This would mean reducing the amount of foods such as cheese, butter and fatty meats that the child consumes. The child should also reduce the amount of salt in her diet by not adding any extra salt or consuming salty foods such as crisps, fish that has been preserved in salt and a majority of the tinned soups on the market.

However, this is an analysis of only three days therefore, this only gives us an insight to her diet. To get a full picture of her diet you could compare more days.

See 'Appendix One' for the 'Diet Analaysis' table.

SECONDARY RESEARCH: The website "Change4Life" encourages parents, as the organisation gives them healthy food ideas, information about portion sizes and ways to cut back on sugar, fat and salt. It is also becoming increasingly used around supermarkets to prompt parents about their food choices (Source D)

The children's television channel "Cbeebies" has various shows such as "I Can Cook" and "Big Cook Little Cook" which teach the children how to eat healthily and so the parents are also viewing the TV shows which encourages them to feed their children more healthily. (Source E)

I found that many supermarkets such as Marks and Spencer's have party platters specifically for children. They contain 4 free-range egg mayonnaise quarters, 4 British chicken no-mayonnaise quarters, 4 cheese quarters, 3 tuna mayonnaise fingers, 3 British ham fingers, and a bag of Percy Piglets. The platters serve 6 to 8 children so I will aim to produce foods that are easy to make in large batches so parents are more encouraged to make them. I found that traditional party foods are scotch eggs, pizzas, sausage rolls, birthday cakes, flapjacks, trifle, cupcakes, ice cream and fruit skewers. This will allow me to choose dishes which can be healthy alternatives to the traditional dishes served at parties. I aim to choose food choices which can be healthy alternatives.

Also it is the parents who are making food choices so we must make sure we influence the parents media so we must make sure we influence the parents.

Whilst looking at the secondary research, I decided to research on young children as I found that it is because parents often cater for young children at parties. This will also allow me to show the healthy alternatives and the food they provide is not always healthy.

PRIMARY RESEARCH: Using "My Supermarket" I compared different sausage rolls on their nutritional content to see which one was lower in salt, calories, sugar, fat and price. I found that Sainsbury's Kids Mini which one has the best portion size for a 5-10 year old. I found that Sainsbury's Kids Mini Sausage Rolls were the lowest in calories, salt and saturated fat. Whereas, Peter's Premier Pork Sausage Rolls were the lowest in sugar and price. The table below is the table I created to record the data I found:

PER 100g	Sainsbury's BGTG Mini Sausage Rolls	Wall's 8 Pork Cocktail Sausage Rolls	Tesco Finest Sausage Rolls	Tesco 6 Pork Sausage Rolls	Ginsters Sausage Rolls	Tesco Sliced Cocktail Sausage Rolls	Peter's Premier Pork Sausage Rolls
Calories	296						
Fat (g)	21.2	21.1					
Saturated Fat (g)	7.4	9.4					
Sugar (g)	1.1	1.3	0.8	1.5	1.4		0.7
Salt (g)	1.1	1.3		1.5			
Price (g)	0.51						

I chose to do a disassembly to see whether the products on the market are healthy because if the foods are healthy, this means parents are being encouraged to feed their children healthily. "My Supermarket" is independent. It states the facts and is unbiased. I also asked a parent to write down what his three year old daughter ate for a week. I then analysed what she ate during a typical three days so I could have a good overview of what foods she would consume each week. I could then work out if her parents were giving her healthy options of food and drink. The graph show what I found in my analysis:

> Suggest 8–10 possible dishes that would meet the brief. This could be presented as a thought shower or a list and doesn't need to take up a whole page as in this example. You could combine it with experimental work linked to the initial ideas.

Healthy Food For Children – Page 3

These ideas are taken directly from a recipe book and are not yet adapted to suit the brief.

IDEAS

SWISS ROLL
Butter for greasing
50g self raising flour
50g caster sugar
2 tbsp warm water
1 tsp vanilla extract
65g strawberry jam
2 eggs
150g double cream
30g strawberry jam

MINI VICTORIA SANDWICH
Cake:
225g butter
225g caster sugar
4 medium eggs
2 tsp vanilla extract
225g self raising flour
Milk, to loosen
Filling:
150g double cream
55g jam

FLAPJACKS
35g wholemeal flour
25g caster sugar
8 tbsp golden syrup
35g oats
25g butter
Butter for greasing

TRIFLE
150g quick set sugar free fruit jelly
25g strawberries
8 sponge fingers
110g custard
75g double cream

MINI CHEESEBURGERS
500g beef mince
4 tbsp mayonnaise
¼ salt and pepper
100g thinly sliced cheddar cheese
1 clove garlic
6 burger buns

PIZZAS
For the toppings:
1 onion
100g tomato puree
150g cheddar cheese
150g mozzarella
For the base:
110g self raising flour
1 tbsp yeast
1 tbsp olive oil
150g warm water

GINGERBREAD MEN
For the biscuit:
100g plain flour
½ teaspoon bicarbonate of soda
1 teaspoon ground ginger
50g margarine
50g sugar
1 teaspoon golden sugar
For the icing:
150g icing sugar
Food colouring
Small amount of water

Healthy Food For Children – Page 4

It is important that your ideas are discussed. Refer back to the aims of the task and the initial brief to ensure that the dishes you select to make are suitable.

DISCUSSION OF IDEAS

Victoria sandwiches are suitable for an occasion like a birthday party where you need a birthday cake. I could also add fruit which will encourage parents to include vitamins and minerals in their child's diet. I could also add fruit which will encourage parents to include vitamins and minerals in their child's diet. Again, the crème fraiche could be added in a thin layer to the centre. This will make the cake moist. Gingerbread men are suitable as they can be made in any shape and this is appealing to children, they are also easy to hold. Pizzas are an easy way to include vegetables in child's diet, they can be colourful and are very child friendly so could be made with children. Producing the base also includes a more complex skill. Burgers are suitable as they can be made smaller, and children enjoy novelty, bite size foods. Also by adding vegetables it increases the nutritional value of the burger and by using lean meat the amount of fat being consumed by the child will also decrease. Also the meat I used was mince meat which is a red meat so the amount of iron in the child's diet will increase. By making sausage rolls I can show skill in the rolling out of the pastry and they are appealing to children. I am also going to add fruits such as apricots to the sausage meat which will increase the amount of fruit in the diet and compliment the meat. Mini trifles are a good idea as they are small portions, are a healthy option instead of cake and can be adapted to suit other occasions and age groups. I believe that flapjacks are a good idea as they can be cut into individual pieces, you can also incorporate fruit into the recipe to increase the nutritional value. I could also use corn oil to grease the tin instead of butter to decrease the amount of saturated fat in the child's diet. The swiss roll shows skill and is an easy way to include fruits into the diet for a parent. I could use crème fraiche instead of double cream and add more fruit.

CRITERIA CHART

The following table rates each of my dishes, according to the criteria of my brief.

	Suitable for a Party	Healthy	Skill	Versatile	Cost	TOTAL
Victoria Sandwiches	2	3	3	2	2	12
Gingerbread Men	3	2	3	2	3	13
Pizzas	3	2	3	3	2	13
Cheeseburgers	3	2	3	3	2	13
Sausage Rolls	3	2	2	3	2	12
Trifles	1	3	2	3	1	10
Flapjacks	2	1	2	3	3	11
Swiss Roll	3	3	3	3	2	14

KEY
1 - Poor
2 - Okay
3 - Good

SELECTION OF RECIPES

I have chosen to make mini burgers, mini victoria sandwiches, gingerbread men, pizzas, sausage rolls, and swiss roll. I chose these dishes as they include high skills, will appeal to children, can be adapted so they will be healthier, they are versatile, they can be used in packed lunches or make portion sizes to feed the rest of the family. They are also good for use at picnics and meals for other days and occasions apart from birthdays, some can be decorated and can be bite sized so they can be held by children. They are individual, interesting shapes, can be adapted so they will be more suitable for children. They are also reasonably healthy options and loved by children. These dishes are also healthy alternatives to traditional foods served at birthday parties. Also the dishes I chose I could easily adapt so that they would encourage parents to feed their children more healthily. They are also reasonably simple dishes so the parents will be able to make them quickly and easily, so therefore they will be more encouraged to make them as they know that they will turn out well. The dishes also have fairly ordinary ingredients which will not cost much so parents from a wide variety of income families will be able to make the dishes if they can afford all the ingredients and will not have to substitute or take out any ingredients. More importantly these dishes are realistic and parents will be encouraged to cook them as they are cheap, easy to produce and can be eaten by the whole family. The dishes also include calcium, protein, carbohydrates and iron which I found was vital to a child's diet.

When selecting dishes it is important to give detailed reasons for choice linked to findings from research and initial aims or criteria.

A criteria chart is a good way of checking the suitability of the dishes, the dishes with the highest marks can then be developed for making.
A 5-point scale could also be applied.

Development or experimental work can be carried out once you have decided on the dishes that you have chosen to make, as in this example; or prior to selecting ideas to help with the decision-making process.

INVESTIGATION
I am going to choose three best ingredients to use in two of my dishes. I am going to create three stuffed crust pizzas and compare the timings taken to cook the pizzas, taste of each crust, nutritional value and look of three different pizzas with three different crusts. I am also going to create three cake recipes. Here, I will compare a victoria sponge mixture, sponge mixture and a fairy cake mixture. I will do this because I would like to make cakes as they can be used as a healthy alternative to a birthday cake.

Experiment One – Mini Pizzas
Sample A: Cheese Stuff Crust
Sample B: Red Peppers and Onions
Sample C: Barbecue Sauce

Experiment Two – Mini Victoria Sponges (healthy alternative to birthday cake)
Sample A - Victoria Sponge Mixture
Sample B - Sponge Mixture
Sample C - Fairy Cake Mixture

METHOD FOR INVESTIGATION WORK

1. Put ingredients for the victoria sponge mixture in a bowl and whisk (3 mins)
2. Put the ingredients for the sponge mixture in a different bowl and whisk (3 mins)
3. Put the ingredients for the fairy cake mixture in another bowl and whisk (3mins)
4. Mix the ingredients for the dough together in a large bowl then knead for 5 minutes. Split into three and roll out into three circles. (7 mins)
5. Put the barbecue sauce in the first crust, cheese in the second crust and red pepper and onion in the final crust. (4 mins)
6. Place pizzas in the oven. (1 mins)
7. Put the mixture from the bowls in paper cake cases and put in the oven. (4 mins)
8. Cook the pizzas and take the pizzas out of the oven when ready. (18 mins)
9. Cook the cakes and take the cakes out of the oven when golden brown (12 mins)
10. Compare the dishes. (5 mins)
11. Wash up. (10 mins)

At home:
Weight out ingredients, Chop red peppers and onions, grate the cheese

KEY:
- Mini Victoria Sandwiches
- Mini Pizzos

Healthy Food For Children - Page 5

Ingredients List

Pizzas
150g cheddar cheese
150g tomato puree
1 whole red pepper
½ large onion
50g barbecue sauce
250g strong white flour
½ teaspoon yeast
150ml warm water
4 tablespoons oil

Victoria Sponge Mixture:
55g butter
55g caster sugar
1 medium egg
2 tsp vanilla extract
55g self raising flour

Sponge Mixture:
25g butter
25g caster sugar
25g self raising flour
Vanilla essence
Pinch of salt
½ medium egg

Fairy Cake Mixture:
35g golden caster sugar
½ medium eggs
25g, self raising flour
7g custard powder or corn flour
35g butter, very well softened

Equipment List:
3 x spoons
1 x balloon whisk
2 x knives
1 x bowl large
3x small bowl
9 x cake cases
4 x baking trays
3 x parchment paper

Hygiene Rules:
- Tie hair back and take jewellery off
- Wash hands and equipment thoroughly

Safety Rules:
- Be careful of the hot water from the kettle when making pizza dough.
- Be careful of the sharp knives when chopping vegetables for the crust.

Conclusion:
I am going to make the victoria sponge mixture as it had a crumbly texture, cooked in only 10 minutes and they browned on top giving them a great appearance. I am also going to make the pizza with the red pepper and onion stuffed crust as it encourages parents to feed their children healthy options of food and drink as they can include vegetables in the crust, without their children realising. They are therefore great for fussy eaters. I may decrease the amount of sugar in the cake to make the mixture healthier as I will be adding sweet fruit such as raspberries and strawberries in the middle of my cake, so the cake itself will not need to be as sweet. This will also make my cakes healthier. The cakes are time saving as I used the all in one method which is a very quick method. Parents could make pizzas with their children and so labour saving for the parents.

Picture on left. From top to bottom: fairy cake mixture, victoria sponge mixture and sponge mixture.

Picture above. From left to right: cheese stuffed crust, barbecue sauce stuffed crust and red pepper and onion stuffed crust.

Relate your experimental work back to the task, suggesting why the changes made have been successful and how it has affected your choice of dishes.

Sequence the planning showing the making of at least 2 dishes. Try to include as much detail as possible. It would be beneficial to include health and safety rules as part of the plan rather than as a separate list.

Healthy Food For Children – Page 6

HEALTH AND SAFETY RULES

1) When cleaning the food processor, take extra care when washing the blade.

2) Make sure when whisking the eggs and sugar that the whisks stay in the mixture the whole time.

3) When taking the swiss roll and the victoria sponges out of the oven make sure you use oven gloves.

4) When cutting the sides of the swiss roll make sure you cut onto a chopping board and be careful not to cut near to your fingers.

5) Make sure that your hair is tied back.

6) Make sure that you remove all jewellery and nail varnish

7) Make sure that you wash your hands.

8) Make sure that when you wash the equipment that you wash it under hot water with washing up liquid, to make sure all bacteria is removed.

9) Make sure that the surfaces are clean and tidy

10) Make sure any thing that has fallen on the floor e.g. containers or grease proof paper, is cleaned up and any spillages are mopped up.

EQUIPMENT
Grease proof paper
Electric whisk
Pastry brush
Large mixing bowl
Small mixing bowl
Metal spoon × 2
Sieve
Swiss roll tin
Sharp knife × 2
Knife × 2
Teaspoon × 2
Cooling rack × 2
Plate × 2
Silicon cases
Food processor
Spatula

Mini Victoria Sandwiches

Swiss Roll

Mini Victoria Sandwiches

Sausage Rolls

PLANNING

11:30 – 11:40 - Collect equipment

11:40 – Turn oven to gas mark 6, 200°c

11:42 – 11:47 - Grease the swiss roll tin then line with grease proof paper

11:47 – 11:49 - Put all ingredients into a food processor and use the mixing function until combined

11:50 – 11:56 - Cream the eggs and sugar until thick

11:56 – 11:58 - Gently fold the sieved flour in using a metal spoon

11:59 – 12:01 - Scoop victoria sponge mixture into a tin

12:01 – 12:15 - Bake for 8-10 minutes or until golden brown and firm

12:01 – 12:16 - Put mixture into silicon cases and place in the oven for 12 - 15 minutes

12:06 – 12:11 - Prepare the butter icing by mixing together the icing sugar and butter in a mixing bowl.

12:11 – 12:15 - Take out of ovens, tip onto sugared grease proof paper once cooked

12:15 – 12:17 - Peel off lining paper

12:17 – 12:19 - Trim the edges of the swiss roll

12:19 – 12:25 - Roll up using the paper to help you

12:15 – 12:20 - Cool on a wire rack

12:20 – 12:38 - Once the victoria sponges have cooled cut in half and spread on the crème fraiche, jam and lay the fruit. Place the other layer back on top.

12:38 – 12:43 - Unroll and spread with jam, crème fraiche and cover in fruit.

12:43 – 13:15 - Re-roll and leave to cool again and clean up

13:15 – 13:30 - Put final products on plates, photograph and then continue to clean.

KEY:
Victoria Sponge
Swiss Roll

Burger

Ginger-Bread Men

Mini Pizza

Colour coding makes it easier to identify each dish.

These dishes have been adapted from the original recipe on page three to make them healthier and suitable for children. For example, I used crème fraiche instead of cream in the swiss roll to make it more moist and healthy. I also added garnishes to the dishes to make them more child friendly for example the facial features and hair on the pizzas. I decided to incorporate fruits and vegetables to improve the nutritional value into the dishes for example apricots in the sausage rolls and onion and red pepper stuffed crust in the pizzas. These all improved the palatability of the dishes and made them healthy.

Summarise the success of the task as a whole.

For Task 2 it is recommended you work out the cost of the dishes individually, and comment on each dish.

Healthy Food For Children – Page 7

COSTINGS
(swiss roll and victoria sandwiches)

225g Butter – 54p
200g Strawberries – £1.99
275g Self-raising flour – 34p
275g Caster sugar – 34p
3 tsp Vanilla extract – 47p
6 Eggs – £1.54
300g Crème fraiche – £1.04
120g Jam – 33p
1 tsp Yeast – 8p
TOTAL – £5.79

Your Shopping Companion

EVALUATION
SUMMARY

On reflection of my practical session, I feel I kept to my timings were realistic. I felt that I was organised and I did not have to go back and get any equipment from the cupboards so I planned well. I also believe that the recipes I chose were suitable for children's parties, as they were made into small portions (finger foods) and when I researched in children's party foods I found that the dishes I had chosen were traditional. After making the dishes, I thought that my dishes could suitably encourage parents to feed their children more healthily. This is because I adapted them to make them cheaper by using ingredients found in an average kitchen. I included a vegetable stuffed crust, the cakes had polyunsaturated spread instead of butter in them and crème fraiche was used instead of cream. I also feel that my decoration choice for the gingerbread men was good as this decreased the total amount of sugar in my recipe. The dishes I made did not need any special skill or equipment, but if no food processor was available the dishes could be made using a bowl and a spoon. I also feel that the dishes are quick to make so this would encourage parents to produce them. The dishes can also be adapted to feed the whole family.

I feel that I could have improved my burgers by using small bread rolls instead of large bread rolls and cutting them into smaller sizes. If I was able to redo my dishes I would have thought more about the icing and decorations for the gingerbread men in order to make them more healthy and appealing. I could have also added more vegetables to my pizzas and use wholemeal flour in the dough instead of white flour.

I think that the costs could have been lowered in order to make my dishes more accessible for different income families but on average they are not too expensive. I feel that many families will be encouraged to use my dishes in order to feed their children healthier foods and drinks. I could have left out the vanilla extract in order to reduce the price but I feel that this added a lot of flavour to the dishes. I could have also used tinned fruit instead of fresh fruit to reduce the overall cost.

STAR DIAGRAMS

Overall I think that my dishes were fairly successful as generally they were healthy and attractive. They were all cooked for the right amount of time so they did not burn and the texture and taste were also good for most of my dishes. They were also suitable for small finger foods and my dish included improvements. I also feel that my dishes included healthy vegetables.

Comment on the taste, texture and appearance of each dish and suggest improvements.

Star diagrams are an excellent way of analysing the sensory qualities of the dishes. Try to choose positive criteria to describe the dishes.

KEY

1 – Poor
2 – Unsatisfactory
3 – Satisfactory
4 – Good
5 – Great

Pizzas

Mini Burgers

Sausage Rolls

Gingerbread Men

Swiss Roll

Victoria Sandwiches

Healthy Food For Children – Page 8

NUTRITIONAL ANALYSIS I have summarised the mini victoria sandwiches and the swiss roll using an "eat well plate" because it is the most well known healthy eating scheme and I could easily categorise the ingredients I used into the sections. For the fruit section, I found that there were two portions of fruits and vegetables included in these dishes. Strawberries and strawberry jam count as one portion, I would not increase the amount of fruit and vegetables in these dishes as it would spoil the texture and I hope the child would eat others throughout the day in a main meal. It is important that the amount of fruits and vegetables are made up in other areas of the diet as they contain vital vitamins that are needed for illness prevention. The parent could make fruit juices or smoothies to increase the amount. I can also see there is a very little amount of carbohydrate and a lot of fats and sugars. This means that the child will be getting a quick burst of energy but little long term, slow release energy. Too much fat can cause obesity so the other meals the child is eating should be low in fat in order to maintain a balanced diet. I would increase the amount of carbohydrates in this child's diet by giving them a high carbohydrate diet for example a cereal such as Weetabix or Shreddies for breakfast. It is important that the child also has a high carbohydrate breakfast in order for them to have energy right the way through the day, as children are very active. This will also discourage them from snacking throughout the day. A way of decreasing the fats and sugars in the dishes would be by using sweetener instead of sugar. My dishes have very little protein, with eggs being the single source. I would advise the parents to provide other party foods rich in protein, for example egg mayonnaise sandwiches or a grilled bacon sandwich. Protein is very important in a child's diet as they are growing and protein is needed for growth and repair of body cells. There is the right amount of dairy produce in my two dishes and this is important as dairy produce provide calcium which is needed for strong, healthy bones and teeth. To ensure that the calcium is being absorbed the parents must ensure that within the child's diet they consume enough vitamin D which is vital for the absorption of calcium. The child will receive vitamin D from the sun but it is also recommended that the parents use margarine instead of butter, as margarine is fortified with vitamin D. Breakfast cereals are also fortified with vitamin D. They could add vitamin D to party foods by making flapjacks as this recipe includes margarine which is fortified with vitamin D. These dishes include enough vitamin C which is needed for the absorption of Iron. It would be recommended that parents give their children a source of iron such as red meat once each week so the child can form healthy red blood cells. I would suggest that parent offers orange juice as a drink at the party to ensure that the child consumes enough vitamin C and a smoothie to ensure that the child consumes enough calcium. It is very important to influence the child's eating habits at this age when they are just starting to choose their own food, in order to make sure they will choose a balanced diet right the way through their lives. The dishes I analysed were all small so were perfect for children, as they like finger foods. The dish that could be improved was the burgers as they did not look as appealing as I would have liked and were slightly too large for a child's portion. I tried to overcome this problem by cutting the rolls out which affected the overall presentation. All dishes met the criteria by being child friendly and encouraging parents to feed the ~~dishes~~ ~~which~~ healthy foods in the dishes.

Comments have been made that are relevant to the target group, 'The Eatwell plate' is a good guide for healthy eating and comparisons but it is not as accurate as using a nutritional analysis program and comparing against the DRVs for the age.

EAT WELL PLATE

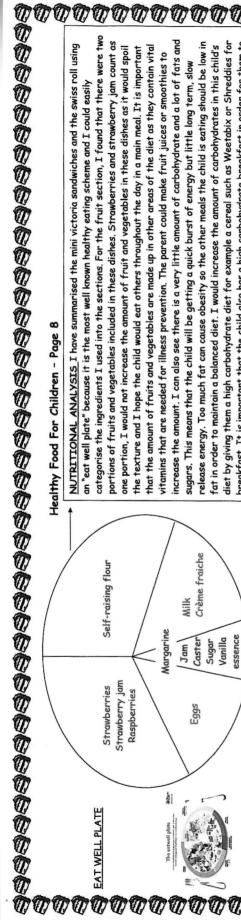

- Strawberries
- Strawberry jam
- Raspberries

- Self-raising flour

- Margarine

- Jam
- Caster
- Sugar
- Vanilla
- essence

- Eggs

- Milk
- Crème fraiche

The eatwell plate

Recommendations:

1. You could accompany the dishes with a side dish to increase the nutritional value and portion size e.g. accompanying the mini victoria sandwiches with a smoothie or the mini burgers with vegetable sticks in replacement for chips.

2. I could try my dishes out at parties to see if the dishes work in the environment I wanted them to.

3. I could ask young children to taste my dishes to see if they would eat them, in order to see if I have made suitable dishes.

4. Use polyunsaturated spread instead of butter at all times to decrease the amount of fat and increase the amount of vitamin D.

5. I could try different fillings for my swiss roll for example mango and passion fruit which introduce variety into the child's diet.

6. I could have interviewed or sent out a questionnaire to parents to find out their views on my dishes before hand. ~~this~~ ~~would~~ ~~have~~

CONCLUSION: Out of the six dishes that I produced the most successful was the mini victoria sponges because they looked appealing, included sources of Calcium, Carbohydrates, Vitamins and Minerals, so they were nutritionally sound. They were small so were perfect for children, as they like finger foods. The dish that could be improved was the burgers as they did not look as appealing as I would have liked and were slightly too large for a child's portion. I tried to overcome this problem by cutting the rolls out which affected the overall presentation.

~~It~~ ~~is~~ ~~important~~ to suggest ~~improvements~~ ~~to~~ ~~all~~ ~~areas~~ ~~of~~ ~~the~~ ~~Task~~ ~~not~~ ~~just~~ ~~your~~ ~~practical~~ ~~work~~ ~~and~~ ~~look~~ ~~at~~ ~~areas~~ ~~that~~ ~~you~~ ~~could~~ ~~develop~~ ~~further.~~

It is important to suggest improvements to all areas of the Task not just your practical work and look at areas that you could develop further.

Research

To help you investigate a topic you will be asked to use both primary and secondary research. Research is only useful when it is collected from reliable sources and is analysed thoroughly.

Primary research

This method of research involves you collecting data for yourself.

It can be collected in one of the following ways.

- Questionnaire

  This involves asking people in your target group for their opinions and/or preferences about your chosen topic.

- Surveys

  These are similar to a questionnaire but instead of asking someone else questions, you are carrying out an investigation for yourself, e.g. surveying the range of cake products available in different supermarkets. You may look at comparing the cost of different products, the nutritional value or the range available.

- Ask an expert

  If you want to know about a topic in detail it may be worth trying to interview someone with specialist knowledge, e.g. asking a chef about developing new dishes for a restaurant, or the head cook in the canteen if you are studying school meals. When carrying out an interview it is important to prepare a list of questions beforehand so that you cover all the points you need to know.

- Existing product analysis

  To help you get a better idea of the types of products already available on the market it is a good idea to carry out some existing product analysis. This involves disassembling a product considering the following points:

  - Name of product.
  - What 'market' has it been made for?
  - How much did it cost to buy?
  - How many portions does the product serve?
  - What are the main ingredients used to make it?
  - How has this product been made/finished?
  - List the good features of the product.
  - List the bad features of the product.
  - What could you do to improve the product?
  - What features of the product would you use in your design?
  - What is the nutritional value per portion?

Writing a Questionnaire

- Before producing your questionnaire you need to identify your target group, this is the group of people that you want to make your product for.

- Think about the number of people you want to answer your questionnaire and if you want a mix of males and females.

- Decide what you want to find out and make sure that the questions are relevant to the topic.

- Make the questions clear and easy to understand, if possible use closed questions having yes/no answers or multiple choice.

- Use open questions, e.g. describe your daily eating habits, when you want more detailed answers to a question.

- After carrying out your questionnaire, present your answers as graphs and draw conclusions about what you have found out.

- Use the results of your questionnaire to help you decide on and develop your ideas.

An 8-point star profile. 5- or 6-point star profiles are also used.

After considering the points above it is also beneficial to carry out some **sensory analysis** on the product you are testing. There are many different tests (which are discussed on pages 170–171) but a **sensory attribute profile** or star chart is most commonly used. To complete the sensory attribute profile, you must choose eight words that could be used to describe the desirable qualities of a product, e.g. colourful, creamy, crunchy. It is important to have a mix of taste, texture, appearance and aroma descriptors if possible.

These qualities are then marked out of 5 (1 being the lowest and 5 the highest).

Primary research is a very important part of your task as it shows that you have found out information for yourself and have been able to evaluate that information. It is important to remember that evaluating and giving an opinion on why you have done something is the key to achieving a good mark in this section.

Secondary research

Secondary research involves looking at information that has already been gathered by someone else, and using that information to help you understand your chosen topic better.

You can research using:

- Books – Gathering information from books can be a very useful method of research, it is important to use a range of books so that you can compare the information. Don't copy information straight from a book, summarise the key points; this shows that you understand the work.

- Websites – Although the Internet is a source of vast amounts of information, it is important that when you are searching websites you choose those which are reliable, and ensure the information is accurate by comparing information from a variety of sites. Like research from books, it is important to summarise and discuss the information rather than copying large sections of text straight from a website.

- Magazines and newspapers – If you can find newspaper or magazine articles related to your topic, it is important to give your opinion of them and say how they are relevant to your research. You may want to put a copy of relevant articles into your appendix, to show where your information has come from.

- Leaflets – As with magazines and newspapers, it may be useful to include leaflets used in your appendix and summarise only the information you feel is relevant to your research.

It is important when you are collecting your information that you use reliable sources and do not copy any work directly, also keep a note of where you get all your information from. Be careful not to insert pages and pages of secondary research. It will be your own summaries and conclusions that will be awarded marks, not the secondary source material.

Evaluating research

When you have collected all your research it is very important to evaluate what you have found out. You need to read all of the articles or books you have found and give your opinion on how the information relates to your topic. You also need to comment on any primary research carried out and give reasons why you had the results you did. For example, you may say that after looking at the results of your questionnaire, you think that many people now eat five portions of fruit and vegetables a day because there is always lots of advertising to encourage people to do this. Evaluating is what ensures you will get the best grades.

Choosing recipes

When carrying out research, it is often common to consider only information to be used in the written investigation of the topic. However, it is also important to research into the recipes you choose to make during the development of ideas section and final making.

When choosing recipes, only use those from reliable recipe books and websites. Your teacher will help you to decide which will be the most suitable.

Savoury dishes

Savoury food is food that is likely to be salty or spicy in flavour rather than sweet, and these foods often form the basis of a main meal, or savoury snack.

Sweet dishes

Sweet foods are usually served as a dessert or as a sweet snack, e.g. as part of afternoon tea. Sweet dishes can range from cakes and biscuits to cheesecakes and mousses.

During the course you will learn how to make a variety of different dishes. You will learn different skills in making these dishes and you will need to show these skills when you choose the recipes for your Task 1 and Task 2. Try and choose dishes that have a range of skills and try to show different skills in each dish.

Savoury and sweet dishes can often combine a range of skills in a single dish, and it is important to be familiar with the skills required when trying out new recipes. When you have mastered the basic techniques you can combine them to make more advanced dishes.

When choosing dishes to cook it is good to have variety, so it may be worth considering making two savoury and two sweet dishes for Task 1. You should aim to show high-level skills where possible. The following list gives you some idea of the skill levels of different dishes.

Higher-level skills:

- Pastry making – choux, short crust, flaky.
- Enriched bread dough.
- Roux-based sauces.
- Decorated cakes and gateaux.
- Complex desserts – soufflé, gelatine set desserts.
- Meringues and pavlovas.
- Meat and fish dishes (using high risk food).

Medium-level skills:

- Vegetable and fruit dishes requiring even sizes, e.g. stir-fry, fruit salad.
- Simple cakes and biscuits – scones, cookies, fairy cakes.
- Basic bread dough.
- Simple sauces.

- Desserts such as cheesecake.
- Dishes made with ready-made puff pastry that only need shaping.
- Simple pasta and rice dishes.

Basic skills:

- Crumbles.
- Pizza with a ready-made base.
- Simple salads.
- Products made using convenience food, e.g. prepared sauce, pastry cases and wraps.

It is useful to carry out a skills checklist on dishes you may decide to make for your practical assessment. This will give you a good idea of the skills you are displaying, and is also a good check on whether you are repeating skills.

An example of a skills checklist for making a beef lasagne:

- Vegetable preparation.
- Handling a high risk food.
- Roux sauce.
- Using hob – sauce making.
- Using oven – baking.
- Garnishing.

You could choose to make your own pasta for the lasagne, which would add additional skills of:

- Pasta making.
- Kneading and shaping.

As part of your research, and to justify your choice for practical assessment, it may be useful to carry out the following type of checklist where you:

- Select dishes suitable for the task.
- List food preparation and cooking skills.

Example of a checklist for cereal-based dishes:

	Handling meat	Chopping	Using the hob	Using the oven	Roux sauce	Blended sauce	Pasta making	Kneading & shaping
Pasta								
Lasagne	✓	✓	✓	✓	✓		✓	
Macaroni cheese			✓	✓	✓			
Spaghetti Bolognaise	✓	✓	✓					
Rice								
Sweet and sour	✓	✓	✓	✓		✓		
Chili con carne	✓	✓	✓	✓				
Curry	✓	✓	✓	✓				
Bread								
Bread rolls				✓				✓
Naan bread				✓				✓
Noodles								
Chow mein	✓	✓	✓					
Stir-fry	✓	✓	✓					

As well as considering the skills used in making the dishes, other considerations are:

- The food must look **colourful and appealing**. When you are making more than one dish, try and use a variety of colours so that they complement each other and look attractive. Garnish savoury dishes with herbs, or add a sauce or side salad to enhance the main dish. When serving sweet dishes, decorate with cream, sauce or fruit to add colour, flavour or texture to the dish.
- The food should be **well presented**; wipe plates clean and choose serving dishes that complement the food you have made.
- The **texture** of the food should be varied, if serving a soft dish such as lasagne, it may be more interesting to serve it with a side salad with a crunchy texture.
- The **taste** of the food is obviously very important to the enjoyment of a dish. Try to make dishes which have a range of flavours, by using different ingredients in each dish, and ensure foods are seasoned when required.
- When serving your dishes, try to make sure you serve them at the correct **temperature**. Hot food should be served hot, and plates should be warmed. Cold food should be kept in the fridge until ready to be served.

Modifying recipes

Once you have had an opportunity to develop your practical skills, you will be able to look at recipes and modify them to suit your Tasks 1 and 2.

You may need to modify recipes for a number of reasons:

- To make them suitable for a special diet.
- To improve the nutritional value.
- To alter the taste, texture or appearance.

Modifying recipes is particularly important when carrying out the experimental work in Task 2. Below are some suggestions of ways you could adapt and trial your dishes.

You want to make a burger that is lower in fat and includes one portion of vegetables

You have decided to use chicken as your meat content because it is low in fat. You have decided to add the following to the basic burger recipe:

- Sample 1: grated carrot
- Sample 2: grated courgette
- Sample 3: grated butternut squash.

To help you decide which flavours will be the most suitable you ask a range of people to carry out sensory analysis on the burgers and record your results. You can then make the most popular dish for your practical work.

You have decided to make a fruit cheesecake; you don't know what colours and flavours will be most attractive to your teenage target group

You have decided on a set cheesecake, you are going to make three individual cheesecakes with different fruit toppings:

- Sample 1: strawberry and kiwi
- Sample 2: blueberry and raspberry
- Sample 3: pineapple and passion fruit.

Ask your target group to comment on the appearance of the dish, give them a small sample of each cheesecake and ask them to rank the dishes in order.

You are trying to develop a vegetarian pie, you have decided it will be made with puff pastry but you are unsure what filling would be most appealing

You are going to use a roux sauce as a base for a filling and want to improve the protein content, appearance, flavour and texture by adding other ingredients.

Add the following to the basic sauce:

- Sample 1: Quorn and mixed vegetables.
- Sample 2: goats' cheese and roasted vegetables.

You can ask your target group to choose their favourite sample and suggest any improvements that could be made.

Planning the practical assessment

Practical skills are not only the skills involved in making the product but also the way you carry out your practical sessions. You will need to show that you can plan your practical successfully before you carry out the practical test.

Organisation is the key. It is very important that you are familiar with each of the stages in your recipes and the order in which you should make your dishes. It wouldn't be very sensible to make a dish that needed to be chilled for an hour last and make a dish that needed to be served hot first.

It is usually necessary to split up your recipes; for example, you may make a sponge first, then whilst it is cooking in the oven, make a spaghetti bolognaise, and then return to adding the filling and decorating the cake once it has cooled. This is called multitasking and at first, it is difficult to master, but will improve with practice.

Make sure that you allow time at the start of your cooking session for preparation prior to cooking. If your area is set up before you start and you have collected all your equipment then you will be more organised during the making.

A time plan will help you to make sure you can complete all the dishes within the time given. When you are completing Tasks 1 and 2 you should aim to complete at least two dishes in each session. The time plan below is an example for making four dishes.

Things to remember when producing your time plan:

In the last column, the following things need to be visible: important points related to health and safety, hygiene, cooking temperatures, etc.

The following outcomes need to be prepared first: bread, pastry, desserts that need to be chilled/set, cakes that need to cool before decorating.

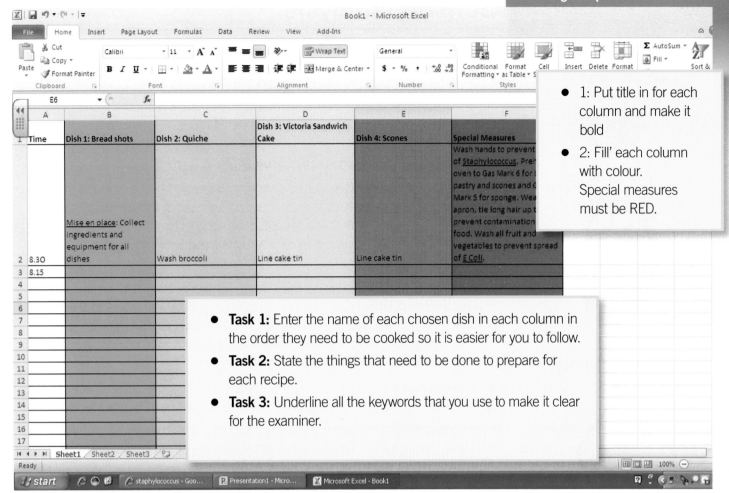

- 1: Put title in for each column and make it bold
- 2: Fill' each column with colour. Special measures must be RED.

- **Task 1:** Enter the name of each chosen dish in each column in the order they need to be cooked so it is easier for you to follow.
- **Task 2:** State the things that need to be done to prepare for each recipe.
- **Task 3:** Underline all the keywords that you use to make it clear for the examiner.

Starting your time plan

When you are producing your time plan you will need to consider the following points:

- Specialist terminology – named processes, e.g. knead, prove, chop, bake
- Timings
- Key temperatures and temperature controls
- Portion control
- Sizes and measurements
- Weighing of ingredients
- Shape and consistency
- Finishing techniques used, e.g. glazing, piping, trimming, decorating, garnishing
- **Personal hygiene,** e.g. **clean** hands
- **Kitchen hygiene,** e.g. **clean** equipment
- **Food hygiene and safety,** e.g. controls preventing contamination, use of food probe
- Safety point for you, e.g. use of oven gloves
- **Accompaniments** – items offered separately to main dish.

Appearance and Colour

Taste and Texture

Smell or Aroma

Activity

Thinking about all the senses, make a list of the words that you could use to describe the following products:

a) Cheese and onion crisps

b) Lemonade

c) Digestive biscuit

d) Lasagne

e) Chocolate sponge pudding.

Sensory analysis

What is sensory analysis?

Sensory analysis is a way of evaluating the taste of a product. The senses play an important part in evaluating the quality of a food product, it is important that food tastes, looks and smells good and has the correct texture.

Who uses sensory analysis?

Food companies use sensory analysis to find out if people like the products they are developing. People have different tastes, so they need to make changes to the ingredients they use in their products so that they appeal to more people. As they make changes they will carry out more sensory analysis until they produce a product they are happy with.

We can use sensory analysis in a similar way in school. If we want to change and develop a product we can ask people to taste the products we make and give their opinions. For example, you may want to develop a new vegetarian product, so you may make a product using a variety of meat replacements and ask people to give their opinion about which one is best.

When developing a new product it is important that you get the views of your chosen target group, e.g. children, teenagers or adults, so you will need to test your dishes on people who are from your specific group.

Setting up sensory analysis

When carrying out sensory analysis it is important that your tasters know what they are tasting, what is expected of them and how to fill in the charts. You must:

- Set up in a quiet area where tasters cannot talk to one another.
- Serve small portions of food in identical, plain containers.
- Serve all samples at the same temperature.
- Allow the tasters to have a drink of water or lime water between each sample to clear their palette.
- Not give too many samples at once as their taste buds can get tired.
- Use random codes for the products to avoid the tasters being influenced by a name, this is called **blind tasting**.

Sensory descriptors

When analysing food products, try to use a range of vocabulary to describe each of the sensory qualities. Use positive words only to illustrate what qualities or attributes you want your product to have. Below are some examples of sensory descriptors:

Taste	Texture	Aroma	Appearance	Sound
Spicy	Moist	Sweet	Colourful	Crunchy
Bland	Soft	Yeasty	Shiny	Sizzling
Sour	Juicy	Spicy	Smooth	Bubbling
Sweet	Crunchy	Citrus	Rough	Popping
Salty	Chewy	Buttery	Uniform	
Fruity	Crisp	Cheesy	Appetising	
Bitter	Smooth			

What test?

When carrying out sensory analysis it is important to choose the test that helps you get the information you are looking for.

Tests can be used to determine how much a product is liked or disliked or to evaluate a specific quality, e.g. saltiness.

Ranking tests

This test allows food to be put into a rank order, either according to how liked a product is or for a specific quality such as sweetness. The taster could be asked to rank in order different flavours of cupcakes, to discover the most popular flavour and to help determine which one will be produced.

Sample	Rank Order
■	3
●	1
★	2

Triangle tests

Triangle tests are carried out to see if testers can identify the odd one out where two products are the same and one is different. This can be used to see if one product is significantly different from the others and is used by companies who want to develop a product similar to others on the market.

WHICH TYPE OF COLA IS SUGAR FREE.
CIRCLE YOUR ANSWER.

△　○　□

Rating tests

Rating tests allow tasters to give samples or qualities a mark on a five- or seven-point scale from 'extreme like' to 'extreme dislike'.

Profiling tests

This type of text is similar to a rating test, but instead of using one quality or overall preference you rate different sensory aspects of the product. Profiling tests are usually produced as a star diagram; the star can have six or eight points depending on the sensory characteristics chosen. Each taster rates the characteristics on a scale of 1 to 5 (1 being the lowest and 5 being the highest). Results from each taster are averaged and then displayed on the star diagram to give a visual profile.

You can use attribute profiles in your Task 1 and Task 2 to evaluate the sensory characteristics of your practical work.

When you are completing your Task 2, you may want to use a ranking test to find out what recipe or flavour is the most popular when you are selecting recipes to develop.

	Tick a statement for each sample		
	BTR	TRZ	XTE
Like extremely	✓		
Like a lot			
Like a little		✓	
Neither like nor dislike			
Dislike a little			✓
Dislike a lot			
Dislike extremely			

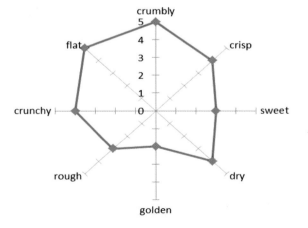

Star diagram for biscuit tasting

Nutritional analysis

Nutritional analysis can be used to look at the nutrients provided by individual dishes as well as being a tool to investigate people's diets.

Dietary analysis can be used to compare the diets of different groups of people with the dietary reference values (DRVs). You may use this in your work to evaluate how healthy someone's diet is or to develop an eating plan for a special diet. It is important once you have recorded the information on a nutritional analysis program that you comment on how suitable the diet is and make suggestions for improvement. You could even put in two sets of data and compare the results from each.

When you evaluate a daily diet is it useful to use the results of food and drink consumed over a three-day period, as this gives a more accurate picture of the range of foods consumed. Where possible, you should try to include a weekend day as eating habits may differ from during the week.

Activity

1. Create a table like the one below to record your diet over a three-day period.

2. State the foods eaten and the amounts

Day	Breakfast	Lunch	Dinner	Snacks
1	150ml orange juice 2 wheat biscuits 150ml whole milk			
2				
3				

2. Use a nutritional analysis program to analyse your diet.

3. Compare the results with the dietary reference values (DRVs) for your age and gender.

4. Comment on the strengths and weaknesses of your diet and suggest improvements.

Extension

5. Make changes to your diet and carry out the nutritional analysis again.

6. Comment on whether these changes have helped you achieve the DRVs for your age and gender.

Activity

1. Choose a recipe that you have made or would like to make.

2. Using a nutritional analysis program, analyse the recipe.

3. Look at the nutrients provided by the recipe. What nutrients is the dish:
   a) high in?
   b) low in?

4. Say whether you think the dish is healthy, giving reasons.

5. Suggest any improvements that could be made.

Nutritional analysis can also be used during the Controlled Assessment task when developing and evaluating products. The nutritional value of food is of great importance to many people when they make their food choices, and analysing the nutrients in different dishes can enable people to make informed decisions.

Once practical work has been completed it is important to analyse the nutritional content of the dishes to ensure that they are balanced. Nutritional analysis programs allow recipes to be input, and carry out a comparison with the dietary reference values (DRVs). This information can often be presented in the form of a graph, which allows for discussion which should be related back to the task.

Once nutritional analysis has been carried out and comments made it is important to discuss any changes that could be made to improve the nutritional value.

The chart on the left shows the percentage of fat provided by banana muffins when compared against the DRVs for both men and women across the different age ranges.

Some nutritional analysis programs will look at each nutrient in a separate graph, others will analyse all the nutrients in one graph.

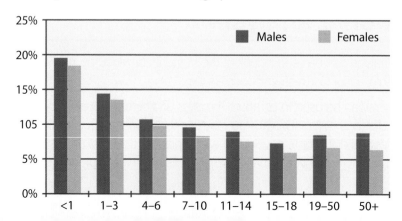

Costing

The cost of ingredients is an important consideration for anyone who is making food, from someone making dinner for the family at home to the production of large quantities of ingredients in a food factory. Many different factors affect the cost of ingredients, such as where the food is purchased, the quality of ingredients and the quantity purchased.

Companies that produce food products are able to buy their ingredients at much more competitive rates as they buy ingredients in much larger quantities that someone who is cooking at home. However, home cooks can reduce the amount they spend on food by:

- Making dishes in large quantities and freezing them to avoid wasting ingredients.
- Taking advantage of offers in the supermarket.
- Buying ingredients when they are in season, so are more widely available.
- Choosing cheaper cuts of meat, and making them into meals with the addition of other less expensive ingredients.
- Use own brand products.

Buying ingredients when you are making dishes from scratch can be expensive but if you are going to make a dish more than once, or other dishes using similar ingredients, it can be cost effective to make dishes, rather than buying them ready prepared or made.

It is important to be aware of the cost of different ingredients; this will help you to make decisions about what ingredients to choose. For example, if a pie recipe requires beef, it is not necessary to use an expensive sirloin steak, where the same flavour could be achieved by using a cheaper cut, such as stewing steak. Visiting the supermarket and looking at the cost of ingredients is the best way of becoming familiar with the prices of different ingredients.

When you make the dishes for your Controlled Assessment tasks, you will need to work out how much they will cost. You can then use this information to compare whether it is better value to make your own or buy a ready-made equivalent dish and make comments in your evaluation. You may also have to work to a budget or have specified economy as part of your criteria in choosing dishes. By costing the ingredients in dishes you will be able to justify your choice.

Activity

1. Use either the formula shown or a spreadsheet with the formula applied to work out the cost of a recipe that you are familiar with such as a Victoria sandwich or scones. Remember to include all of the ingredients.

2. Compare the cost with a similar product that is available to buy ready-made in a shop or restaurant. Comment on whether you think your dish is good value for money. Give reasons for why you think it is cheaper or more expensive to make your own.

Calculating the cost of a recipe

To work out an accurate cost of dishes you make you need the following information:

- Cost of ingredient used
- Amount of ingredient in the packet (g/ml)
- Amount of ingredient used.

You can use the following formula to work out the cost of the ingredients used:

Cost of pack (£) ÷ Amount in pack (g/ml) × Amount used (g/ml) = Cost of ingredients

You can use a table like the one below to record the information and then calculate the cost or you can use a spreadsheet to work out the formula if you have access to a computer.

Ingredient	Amount used	Cost of pack	Amount in pack	Total cost

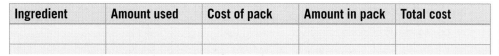

Examination Advice and Technique

The written examination will test your knowledge about what you have learned during the course. The examination will test you on the four units of learning:

1. Nutrition, diet and health.
2. Factors affecting consumer choice.
3. Changes that take place during storage, preparation and cooking of food.
4. Food hygiene and safety.

It is important that you revise thoroughly and learn all the information.

General examination advice

- Read the instructions on the front page of your exam paper.
- Read questions carefully, at least twice, and make sure you know exactly what you have been asked to do.
- Underline or highlight key words.
- Study the marks given for each question or part of a question. This will give you an idea of how many points or facts to write.
- Essay-type answers will need a little planning. Brainstorm or write down a rough outline before writing your answer in sentences.
- Familiarise yourself with command words in the questions.

Top tip

Put a pencil cross through your rough plan once you have finished. The examiner can see that you have planned carefully.

If you happen to run out of time, you may be awarded marks just for the plan.

Activity

Match the following command words to their meaning. Answers are given overleaf.

Analyse   Assess   Describe   Discuss   Explain   Evaluate   Identify   State.

Key word	Description or what it means you should do
1.	Write down a list.
2.	Write clearly but briefly.
3.	Give details about something written down in a few sentences, e.g. how something works or what it looks like.
4.	Identify a point, write down the meaning of it clearly, then follow it with reasons to show that you understand it.
5.	Separate a topic into its various parts in order to be able to identify and explain it.
6.	Assess a topic and say why it is important or what you have learned from it.
7.	Consider, weigh up, make a judgement about a topic.
8.	Write about all aspects of a topic, including advantages and disadvantages, or arguments for and against.

Types of questions

Structured questions

These give you some kind of information such as a diagram, a food label, or a recipe. You are then asked specific questions. There are spaces for you to write the answers and the marks awarded are placed in square brackets next to the questions. The amount of space provided will give you an idea about the amount of detail you should provide in your answer.

Here are some examples:

---

1. The following is a basic bread recipe.

250g strong flour
1 level teaspoon salt
½ sachet quick acting yeast
150ml water
1 tablespoon oil

Method
1. Put flour, yeast and salt into bowl.
2. Add warm liquid and oil. Mix into dough.
3. Knead firmly. Shape into a loaf, place in tin and leave to rise until doubled in size.
4. Bake in a hot oven for about 20 minutes, then reduce the temperature to finish the cooking.

a) Explain the role of the following ingredients in the making of bread: [2]
   - Strong flour
   - Yeast

b) Give **two** reasons why the dough is kneaded. [2]

c) Explain what happens during the baking of the bread. [4]

---

2. a) Study the following pictures.
   Tick the boxes to show the foods that are high in salt. [2]

☐   ☐   ☐

b) Give **one** reason why salt needs to be reduced in the diet. [1]

c) Suggest **two** alternatives to salt when flavouring food. [2]

> **Top tip**
> - Look at the words in the questions.
> - Learn key words and terms.
> - Practise spelling key words.

3. Match the food to the section on the **Eatwell plate.** [3]

(One has been completed for you.)

| tuna | doughnut | spaghetti | tomato | natural yogurt |

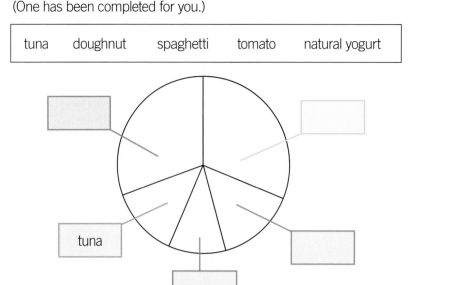

tuna

4. The cheese scones in the picture are made with the following ingredients:

| self-raising flour | margarine | cheese | milk |

Function	Ingredient
Flavour	
Bulk	
Shortening	Margarine
Binding ingredients together	

a) Match the ingredient to the function. (One has been completed for you.) [3]

b) Explain how you would achieve a quality result when making a batch of scones. [6]

Free response questions

These types of question ask you to write about a specific topic. Your answer should include facts, examples and opinions. These types of question often include command words such as assess, describe, discuss, explain or evaluate.

Here are some examples:

1. Despite television cookery programmes being popular, research suggests that many people still do not prepare home-cooked food.

a) Explain, with reasons, why many people are still buying ready prepared foods. [5]

b) Discuss how labour-saving equipment can encourage people to cook at home. [5]

2. You have been asked to write a leaflet giving advice to parents on how to promote and maintain a healthy lifestyle. Discuss the information you would include in the leaflet. [8]

3. Food choice has been increased by current developments such as ethical, organic, functional and GM foods.

   a) Discuss the range of foods available as a result of current developments. [6]

   a) Assess the factors that could influence the inclusion of these foods in family meals. [6]

4. a) Describe ways in which supermarkets attract customers to buy their products. [4]

   b) Discuss the benefits of shopping for food 'online'. [4]

The following three sample answers to the question will give you an idea of how the free response questions are marked and why it important to identify a point and follow it with reasons to show that you understand it. Good answers show understanding of the question and also that the relevant information has been given in the answer.

Question

Different protein foods 'complement' each other. **Explain** why it can be beneficial to include a **mixture** of protein foods in the diet. [6]

Mark scheme

Credit a response which makes reference to the following:

- HBV – animal source
  Contain the essential amino acids
  Named sources – meat, fish, milk, eggs, cheese, soya
- LBV – vegetable / plant
  Do not contain the essential amino acids
  Named sources – nuts, pulse vegetables, cereals, seeds
- Specific examples of how protein foods complement each other, e.g. beans on toast, lentil soup with bread roll
- Reference to soya as a plant source containing HBV
- Reference to one amino acid making up for the loss or compensation for another missing amino acid
- Reference to cost benefits of mixing HBV protein foods and LBV protein foods.

Top tip

- Watch your timing! Leave plenty of time for the essay-type questions.
- Keep referring back to the question.
- Keep your answer focussed.
- Write clearly, without repeating what you have already said.
- Remember, you will be marked on the quality of your written communication.

Answers to Activity on p174

1 Identify
2. State
3. Describe
4. Explain
5. Analyse
6. Evaluate
7. Assess
8. Discuss

Award:

0–2 marks for a basic response which makes little reference to the complementary action of protein.

3–4 marks for a good response with **some examples**. Writing is well structured and clearly expressed with use of some specialist terminology.

5–6 marks for an excellent response with **specific examples**. Writing is well structured and clearly expressed with appropriate use of specialist terminology.

Award maximum 2 marks for answers that refer only to the functions of proteins in the diet.

Answer A

Functions of protein

No reason given

Question not focussed on fat

Question not focussed on vegetarian diets

Question not focussed on vegan diets

Protein is an essential part of a balanced diet. It is needed for growth and repair of body cells. It can be found in food such as ham, which contains iron which keeps your red blood cells healthy. It is important to include a mixture of protein foods because it would harm your health if you only ate red meat. Protein is also found in eggs and milk. Milk and eggs also contain fat which is needed for a healthy, balanced diet. It is used to insulate the body and is the body's last resort of food. If you were a vegetarian you could not eat meat so it is important to eat milk and eggs for protein. If you were a vegan, you would have to eat soya which is the plant source of protein.

Award 2 marks

Answer B

Reference to LBV proteins, with examples

Reference to HBV proteins with examples

Some indication that there is a difference, reference to cost

It can be beneficial to include a mixture of protein foods in the diet because there is a wide range of foods with different types of protein, for example you can have low biological value protein such a bread, nuts, oats and high biological value proteins such as meat, fish, cheese, milk. Eating both of these would be good because they have different values and the cost is also different.

Award 4 marks

Answer C

Reference to amino acids

Shows understanding

Reference to HBV with examples

Reference to LBV with examples

Good examples of complementary action of proteins

It can be beneficial to include a variety of protein foods in the diet because you can obtain the full range of amino acids. Animal protein products, e.g. meat and eggs, will provide all the essential amino acids which the body cannot produce itself. These foods are said to have high biological value. Eating a range of other protein foods, e.g. nuts, peas, bread, will provide the non-essential amino acids, said to have low biological value. The body is able to produce these. Eating a wide variety and a mixture of LBV foods can help you obtain the full range. Two types of LBV proteins can complement each other. Examples are beans on toast, rice with peas.

Award 6 marks

Here are some other exemplar questions and some answers for you to look at:

1. a) To ensure a child's health and safety there are certain foods a parent should avoid giving their child.

   Complete the chart below, giving reasons why these foods should be avoided.

   (The first one has been completed for you.) [4]

Food	Reason to avoid
Salt	Can affect a child's kidneys
Nuts	
High fibre food	
Sugary foods	
Uncooked eggs	

   > This is a two-part question. Often candidates miss out the second part and can only get half the marks.

   b) Explain what is meant by the following conditions and suggest how they may be controlled through diet:

   i) Diabetes. [2]

   ii) Coeliac disease. [2]

2. Eating a well-balanced diet is important for a young child.

The eatwell plate

Use the eatwell plate to help you get the balance right. It shows how much of what you eat should come from each food group.

Fruit and vegetables

Bread, rice, potatoes, pasta and other starchy foods

Meat, fish, eggs, beans and other non-dairy sources of protein

Foods and drinks high in fat and/or sugar

Milk and dairy foods

> This needs more detail than 'healthy' for 2 marks.

> Think about how to make food fun.

   a) What is meant by a *balanced diet*? [2]

   b) Explain why it is important for a child to eat a well-balanced diet. [4]

   c) A recent survey found that one in twenty children refuses to eat, which can cause great anxiety. Suggest ways in which this problem can be overcome. [6]

3. Healthy eating habits should be established in early childhood.
   Discuss this statement. [10]

Introduction shows you understand why healthy eating is important.

Shows understanding of the different nutrients and why children need them (it doesn't matter what adults need for this question).

Identify the problems caused by poor eating habits.

Make sure the end of your answer links back to the question.

Children need a healthy diet to ensure they get all the nutrients they need to grow and develop properly. If they have a wide range of foods in sensible amounts, they should have the right proportions of nutrients. The eatwell plate is a good example of the type of balanced diet that most people should aim for. Children should be encouraged to eat three meals a day, with healthy snacks in between. They should aim for five or more portions of fruit and vegetables every day to make sure they get all the vitamins and minerals they need for growth and to prevent illnesses. Fruit and vegetables also contain fibre to prevent constipation. Main meals should contain protein which the child needs for growth, and enough carbohydrate to give the child energy to play. They also need calcium to develop strong bones and teeth while they are still growing.

Children under 5 do not need to have reduced fat foods such as skimmed milk, because they need the fat to give them energy. However, high fat foods such as crisps and chips should be limited as they do not provide other valuable nutrients. Sweets and sugary drinks should only be given occasionally because of the risk of developing tooth decay. A diet which is high in fat, sugar and salt puts the child at greater risk of developing food-related illnesses as they get older. For example, too much fat and sugar can lead to obesity, heart disease and type 2 diabetes. Too much salt can lead to high blood pressure. All of these can result in reduced life expectancy.

If a child gets used to eating healthy meals and snacks from a young age, they are more likely to continue to have a healthy diet in later life. If they are given the opportunity to try lots of different foods when they are young, they should be willing to eat a wide range as they get older. Bad habits are difficult to break so it is best to give healthy food as soon as a child begins weaning so that they don't develop a taste for foods which could do them harm if eaten in large quantities.

This answer would get full marks because it contains all the relevant information in a logical order.

In high-mark questions like this you will be assessed on your ability to write clearly and follow rules of spelling, punctuation and grammar, so it is a good idea to plan before starting to write.

Activity

Read the following question and mark scheme and then read the two answers to the question.
Award each a mark and give reasons why you have awarded these marks.

Question

Explain how the loss of water-soluble vitamins can be reduced when preparing and cooking broccoli. [4]

Mark scheme

Credit an answer which makes reference to the following points:

- Naming the water-soluble vitamins as C and B group
- Not preparing too early before cooking / not soaking in water
- Even-sized florets
- Break into florets with fingers
- Use the stalk because it is high in vitamins

If boiling the broccoli:

- Boiling water before cooking
- Small amount of water
- Use the liquid for sauce or gravy because vitamins leach into the cooking water
- Cook until crunchy / do not overcook / short cooking time
- Steaming or microwaving as a method of cooking with reasons why – no water used, vitamins sealed in
- Stir-frying as a suitable method because vitamins are kept in the broccoli
- Serving straight away / do not keep warm for long

Award

0–1 marks for a very basic response with reference to one point in the mark scheme.

2–3 marks for a basic response showing some understanding and reference to a few points.

4 marks for a detailed response showing good understanding and covering several of the points listed.

Answer A

You can preserve the loss of water-soluble vitamins by cooking the broccoli in as little water as possible and for a short time. Do not overcook. Steaming the broccoli is best because there is no contact with the water so less vitamins B and C are lost. When preparing the broccoli, wash quickly and do not leave too much time before cooking, and eat straight way after cooking. Also break into even-sized pieces so that all the broccoli is crunchy when cooked.

Answer B

You could cut off bits you don't want then put into a saucepan with as little water as possible. Put the lid on so no water-soluble vitamins will be lost through the water vapour in the steam. Cook at a low temperature and not for too long. This will allow the goodness to stay in the broccoli.

Practise past questions to help you improve on timing and to help you to become familiar with the command words used in questions.

Make sure that your answers are relevant and that you have checked whether you have answered all the questions to the best of your ability.

Revise thoroughly and remember that examiners are on your side – they want to give you marks if at all possible – but you have to earn them.

Index